SHADOWLight

FREEMAN PATTERSON

SHADOWLight

A PHOTOGRAPHER'S LIFE

A Phyllis Bruce Book
HarperCollins*Publishers*Ltd

For André and Parker, whose love and friendship brighten my life

For Gordon, Laura, and Stephen, who are making their best dreams happen, and for their parents, Doris and John, who care about ultimate things

SHADOWLIGHT: A PHOTOGRAPHER'S LIFE

Copyright © 1996 by Freeman Patterson.
All rights reserved. No part of this book may be used or reproduced
in any manner whatsoever without prior written permission
except in the case of brief quotations embodied in reviews.
For information address HarperCollins Publishers Ltd,
Suite 2900, Hazelton Lanes, 55 Avenue Road,
Toronto, Canada M5R 3L2.
http://www.harpercollins.com
First Edition

A CIP record for this title is available from the National Library of Canada.

ISBN 0-00-255075-X

Design: V. John Lee
Editor: David Kilgour

Printed and bound in Canada

ACKNOWLEDGEMENTS
With deep appreciation to Aaron M., Colla S., Kevin L., Lynda T., Phyllis B.,
and Tineke H. for your unique contributions to this book and to my life, and
with special thanks to friends, relatives, and acquaintances who read and
commented on various chapters of the manuscript.

   And, of course, with a fond pat on the head for Tosca.

Front cover: Interior of abandoned house, Kolmanskop, Namibia.
Opposite title page: Abandoned house, Kolmanskop, Namibia.
Page 5: Sunset over the Andes, southern Argentina.
Page 6: Sculpted ice, Alexandria Fiord, Ellesmere Island, Nunavut, Canada.

Contents

Preface

This book is neither a memoir nor a comprehensive retrospective of my work as a photographer. It is, rather, a kind of self-portrait, complete with wrinkles, and an attempt to make sense of the forces, internal and external, that have shaped my life and my work, which are impossible to separate.

Two significant challenges became evident to me early in the writing process and commanded my attention until the end. One was deciding what would be relevant to people who might read this book. I continually fought the temptation to be overly personal, to provide details that were of interest to me, but which even the most patient reader would eventually find collectively boring. When I failed, my editor was not slow to discourage my navel-gazing.

The other, and greater, challenge was to be honest—both in what I said and in what I left out. Time and again I succumbed to the tendency to portray myself, inaccurately, in a favourable light, and had to re-examine not only what I perceived to be the truth, but why I perceived it to be true. Sometimes, the re-evaluation of a situation or a perception caused me to lean too far in the other direction, and I would be tempted to omit material that was accurate, but which I felt might be construed as self-indulgent. The balancing act in which I found myself engaged taught me a great deal about polarities, a subject I write about in "Through the Looking-Glass."

I have arranged text and images mainly according to thematic preoccupations and passions that emerged as I thought, wrote, and looked at thousands of pictures I have made over the last thirty years. The result is perhaps neater, tidier than the reality from which it is distilled. In making my choices, I had to do what any curator must—discard, often with regret, many images and subjects that I cherish. I have chosen not to indicate the year in which each colour photograph was made, because in my view this would be confusing. I believe that there is continuity in my personal growth and in its reflection in my images; however, this general or overall process, when examined internally, is full of shadow and light, false starts and periods of regression, as well as sudden leaps forward and periods of sustained development. That's life, or at least, my life.

Freeman Patterson
Shamper's Bluff
New Brunswick
February 1996

BEGINNINGS

YOU WILL NOT FIND GREY'S MILLS, NEW BRUNSWICK, ON ANY MAP OF CANADA. Nor will you find Gorham's Bluff and Shamper's Bluff, which project out into the St. John River's Belleisle Bay immediately to the north. But, if you have a very detailed map and a bit of luck, just to the south you might find Long Reach, named after the long, straight stretch of water that gives sailors a clear view all the way from Belleisle Bay to Harding's Point, not far from Saint John. In the 1940s, when I was a child, the people who lived in these sparsely populated communities on the eastern side of the river made their living from farming, lumbering, and fishing, and from an early age I was expected to do my part.

From the highest field on our Grey's Mills farm, I could gaze thirty or forty kilometres up and down the river valley. I was there in haying season, which began late in June, turning newly mown grass with a pitchfork or a horse-drawn tedder, or loading hay onto a wagon while banks of towering cumulus clouds began to build high above the hills across the silver-blue water. I was there at dawn, pulling mustard weeds from a field of oats while far below me a vast sheet of mist shimmered gold in the morning light and obscured the river from my view. I climbed the hill in December to search for a Christmas tree, a favourite adventure, when the river was a wind-patterned tapestry of grey ice, snowdrifts, and patches of black, open water that flowed through a gap in the distant hills far into my imagination.

This visual paradise resonated with sounds and fragrances that linger in my memory—the wind-chiming of the forest after an ice storm, the soft rustle of dry grasses chafing in a breeze, the merry pandemonium of birdsong in spring, the spicy aroma of hay-scented ferns crushed between my fingers,

Morning mist over Kingston Creek, near Grey's Mills, New Brunswick.

the sweet, pungent stench of manure spread on gardens prior to ploughing, the lilt of clover and honey in the air, and the rich mustiness of leaves rotting in autumn. Its place in my soul is indelible, not only because its sensual beauty was so all-pervading, but also because my sister, Doris, is four years younger than I, and for the first few years of my life the difference in our ages meant that we did not experience it together. So the trees, rocks, brooks, birds, and every other natural thing became my peer group and my closest friends.

My childhood ended when I was eight—the year my father informed me that, from then on, he would wake me every morning at 5:00 A.M. "to help out in the barn." We had a herd of about thirty milking cows, another twenty to thirty "young cattle," pigs in varying numbers, and a large flock of laying hens.

In the arms of my mother, Ethel Patterson, 1938.

My father, Gordon Patterson, pulling me on a toboggan, 1939.

On my first Harley, 1941.

For the next ten years, until I left home for university just before my eighteenth birthday, the schedule of my days was close to being utterly predictable, varying only slightly with the seasons, and sometimes with the weather. Up at five to feed the animals, help with the milking, and clean the stables. Breakfast at eight. School at nine. Home at four. As I grew older there were more chores in the fields, in vegetable gardens, or around the barns, until the evening barnwork, which was the same as the morning's. After all that there was schoolwork. There were lessons to prepare every night, but I completed them faithfully without any coercion, because in the world of books I found my freedom. Things happened in books and at school. No two days were ever the same. So I threw myself into reading, writing, and arithmetic with a passion. I was unbeatable at spelling. And I had the opportunity to play. I loved softball and soccer. One of the great moments of my young life was scoring a goal in the first soccer game I played as a member of the high-school team, and being carried aloft off the field by my teammates. (The fact that there were only about thirty of us in the high school and more than half were girls virtually assured me a place on the team.) But these things are relative. I was only in grade nine and had just come from a one-

When I was a child, farm families thought twice before tearing down an old house, especially if the building could be put to use as a storage shed or a home for chickens or pigs.

room school where the only teacher taught all eight grades. This school had six teachers and twelve grades.

It wasn't that I hated the farm or the work; in fact, I loved both. The fields and forests were a sort of heaven for a child and, while the work was long, often hard, and sometimes very tedious, cows and pigs and hens made for very good company. I don't have a bad word to say about any of them, and remember many with great fondness. Besides, they taught me a lot— especially about how to get along with neighbours (no pig ever had a serious altercation with a cow, for example), and about being grateful for what you have, even when you are endeavouring to get more.

What bothered me about my life—in fact, affected me seriously in the long run—was the control. There is a difference between guiding a child and controlling a child, but my father did not recognize the distinction. Although he spanked me occasionally, his main instruments of control were to keep me busy and to tolerate no dissent. As a result, I was an extremely well-behaved child.

The white flowers and emerging pinkish leaves of bilberry trees signalled spring's certain arrival in New Brunswick, usually around the middle of May.

At about the age of ten, I decided to make a flower garden just outside our dining-room windows, where it could easily be seen from inside the house. It was a humble effort the first year, consisting mainly of a bed of nasturtiums, but every year after that I became a little more creative and ambitious. The catalogue from Dominion Seed House always arrived in January, when snow and cold were powerful incentives to plan a garden. I remember lying in a hayloft on a Sunday morning studying the colourful illustrations and reading the descriptions of perennials and roses over and over again, calculating what I could afford to buy, then sketching out beds and paths on pieces of scrap paper. The gardens of my imagination were amazing—full of ever-blooming flowers of every hue and shade, and magically free of weeds. Finally, in February, I placed my order. A parcel containing the seeds arrived soon afterward, followed in April by gladioli bulbs; roots of phlox, peonies, and iris; and any shrubs I'd ordered. From that moment on I spent every free moment in my garden—digging, planting, weeding, staking, and most of all just looking. It was so much more exciting than my father's vegetable gardens with their long straight rows of turnips, carrots, parsnips, peas, potatoes, and corn, where I had to spend far more time weeding and harvesting than I ever could spend with my flowers.

The spring before I went to university I acquired an "old-fashioned" shrub rose that I badly wanted, carefully chose a site for it, and tended it so well that it rewarded me with many beautiful blossoms that first year. I had visions of how spectacular it would be in two, five, and ten years' time. When I returned home after spring examinations the following year, I noticed that the rose bush was gone, and immediately asked my mother what had happened to it. "Oh," she replied, "I thought you'd be upset by that. Your father dug it up. He said that it might spread."

If it is true that children understand the concept of God and feel the presence of the divine first through their parents, it is small wonder that I initially experienced God as a being who created things (a kind of super-farmer) and condemned sinners (everybody who disagreed with him). Of course, God was male. Preachers at the little church nearby reinforced the concepts of authority, sin, and judgement with such guilt-inducing certainty

The members of the MacDonald Consolidated School soccer team, 1952. (I'm on the right.)

Showing a Holstein cow at the 4-H show, Hampton, New Brunswick, 1954. (The cow won second prize.)

Every family in the community had a
flower garden of sorts, almost invariably
planted and cared for by the women, who
often found it difficult to maintain
because of their heavy workload and also
because the men were sometimes less
than careful about where they ploughed,
mowed, released animals, or parked farm
machinery.

that for a few years I think I functioned as a person completely out of
touch with his feelings.

So life in my personal garden of Eden was far from idyllic. In order to
please both my biological father and my "heavenly" one, I had to bury essential aspects of myself. Eventually realizing that my father had imprinted
me with his own unexamined anger and that I was replicating his behaviour,
I began the task of emotional re-excavation in order to deal with my negative
emotions. Only when I had completed much of the digging, and my father
was very old, did I come to understand what a wounded man he was and how
his need to control those close to him was his way of covering up a profound
lack of self-esteem that he could never admit, even to himself. As my fear of
him gradually subsided and my sympathy grew, there were a thousand questions that I would like to have asked him, but never could.

There were many wives and children in the string of communities who
experienced similar relationships with their husbands and fathers. On the
whole these men were courteous, honest people who helped their neighbours
and provided the material goods their families required, but even at an early

▶ The first flowers I ever grew were
nasturtiums, annual plants that were
easy to care for and came in a wide
range of bright colours. Within a couple
of years I had expanded my floral
repertoire to clarkia and lavatera, which
few had ever heard of.

age I sensed a parallel between the way they treated their family members and their efforts to manage or control nature. Although all of them farmed or lumbered, none displayed a genuine closeness to nature or an appreciation that every species is important to maintaining the health of the natural family. On the other hand, I felt very close to nature—indeed, my childhood bonding with natural things helped me survive my early emotional and religious turmoil, and revealed the natural world to me as a place for healing.

My mother, a woman from the city, was the agent of revelation. Her quiet influence had sensitized me to the amazing world around me, enabling me to marvel at the banks of cumulus clouds above the distant hills when I was loading hay, to pause while weeding the oat field in order to watch the golden mist moving through the valley, to feel pleasure at the ice patterns in the frozen river. Her constant delight in the way flocks of birds wheeled and turned (performance art), in the colour patterns of feathers and flowers (visual art), and in pictures of places she had never been and never would be affected me far more deeply than I knew. The fact that these things didn't matter to my father meant that, for the most part, she could indulge her caring for them without his even being aware of what she was doing. The longer she lived on the farm, the more she created her own world, as it were, and in doing so she gave me permission to build mine.

My mother had an innate sense of the importance of craft to art, which she exercised in the two aesthetic pursuits available to her. One was ongoing: like her mother before her, she grew geraniums on east- and south-facing windowsills, watering, fertilizing, and repotting them in a sequence and at times that revealed the most careful observation of the plants' needs. As a result, the windows of our home were almost always full of riotous red, salmon-pink, rose-pink, and occasionally pure white blossoms.

And, she trimmed our Christmas tree. There was never another tree in the community that could match its beauty. Mother liked a tree that was a tall triangular shape of good proportions and not too bushy, because she knew that the secret of decorating magic into a tree was in not hanging all the ornaments on the tips of the branches. There had to be flashes of mysterious light and colour emanating from the interior of the tree and from the

In the days before hydro poles, all the roads in the community looked more or less like this. Because traffic was infrequent, they were great places for sledding in the winter, for bicycling in the other seasons, and for evening strolls. Years later, when I had moved back to the area, I met one of my favourite neighbours, by now in her eighties, walking along a gravel road, enjoying the autumn colour. Knowing that I travelled frequently in the course of my work, she was surprised to see me, and greeted me with, "Why, Freeman, it's good to see you. Tell me, are you home or away?"

My mother noticed the colours of faded grasses, frost on cabbage plants, and similar things, and commented on them. Her appreciation of quiet beauty was one of her greatest legacies to my sister and me.

far side, nearest the wall. After she had hung all the ornaments—with the most thoughtful consideration of their location on the tree relative to their size, shape, colours, and the position of other ornaments—she draped the tree with shimmering silver icicles, one at a time, choosing the placement of each as carefully as that of the ornaments, all to enhance the tree's majesty and depth. When electricity finally came to our rural community, she was the only person who did not rush out to buy Christmas-tree lights. She sensed that the two kinds of magic would not mix, and she preferred the subtle and mysterious to the obvious. Learning from her, as I surely did, I quickly realized that the bright illumination from other electric lights in the room diminished the effect she had laboured so hard to create, and insisted that our living-room be illuminated at Christmas only by kerosene lamps or candles.

A few days before my eighteenth birthday I left home for university. Nobody was ever more eager to go than I. For the previous three years I had been devouring university calendars, comparing programs and courses, and attempting to discern the ambience of each institution. Eventually I settled

▶ Ice storms were never much of a problem in the days before electrical wires and "improved" roads. About the worst that could happen, and only if I wasn't careful, was an unexpected slide on my bum. And that was usually fun! Besides, when the sun came out, the world was utterly transformed—a place of magic.

on Acadia University, in Nova Scotia's Annapolis Valley, largely on the basis of its liberal-arts program and its beautiful setting, where my meagre personal savings, scholarships, and wages from working (as a waiter, as an aide to a fellow student who was confined to a wheelchair, and as a marking assistant to professors of English and philosophy), enabled me to pay my own way.

My grades were good the first year, and better the second, so at the beginning of my third year I decided to switch from the regular BA degree program in English to an honours program in philosophy, with minors in English and biology. About the same time I became increasingly involved in extracurricular activities—especially inter-varsity debating and theatre. My acting debut was as Prince Florizel in Shakespeare's *The Winter's Tale*, in which I replaced the original prince, who had flunked his mid-year exams. Later on, as John of Gaunt in *The Tragedy of King Richard II*, I had a heart attack on several successive evenings and each time died magnificently in full view of the paying customers—only to be promptly resurrected as a bishop. (In 1989, while I was being conferred an honorary doctorate by Acadia, I suddenly realized that the ceremony was taking place on the very spot where I had succumbed on numerous occasions thirty years earlier, and for a wicked moment I contemplated trying it one more time.)

The discipline I had learned on the farm paid off handsomely at university. The more extracurricular activities I became involved in, the better I organized my time. The better I organized my time, the higher my marks. During my third year I applied for and won a World University of Canada scholarship to spend the summer in what was then Yugoslavia. I was beside myself with excitement and, like millions of others visiting Europe for the first time, I bought a camera before I left, and I took a lot of pictures. I found that I enjoyed working with a camera, that it focused my seeing and gave me the added pleasure of knowing that, when I returned home, I could share what I had seen. But this was not to be. Only when I had my films processed back in Canada did I discover that the camera was defective and that, in fact, I had exposed no film at all. My emotions sank to a low that matched in depth the height of my excitement about the trip itself. Yet the

With my sister, Doris, a few days before I left for Acadia University, September 1955.

loss was not a complete one, because I'd enjoyed the picture-taking too much to forget about it. So I had the camera repaired, and used it around the university and elsewhere whenever I could afford to buy some film.

In my senior year at Acadia, two of my professors nominated me for a Rockefeller fellowship. About seventy of these were awarded annually on a competitive basis to students in the arts and sciences graduating from North American universities who were not contemplating a career in church ministry but who would be willing to spend a fully funded year at a school of theology and consider the possibility. To this day I don't know why my professors thought I was an appropriate candidate, but I won a fellowship. I applied to both Yale Divinity School, and Union Theological Seminary on the Columbia campus in New York City, which along with Harvard were considered to be the best theological schools on the continent. I ended up at Union, and there began a chain of events that was to alter the direction of my life forever.

Union required all entering students to undergo extensive psychological and vocational testing. In the consultations that followed, my adviser revealed to me that I showed, above all else, a very strong thrust towards the arts. I was stunned! As I had come from a farm background where life's least concern was aesthetic impulse, this was a career possibility that had never so much as crossed my mind. At the time I made no connection between the test results and my mother's Christmas tree, or my flower garden, or my camera. So I buried the information for a while, and busied myself with my required courses in Old Testament, New Testament, Systematic Theology, Practical Theology, and Philosophy of Religion. If my father believed that everybody should stand on his or her own two feet, then the professors at Union believed that everybody should fly. The workload was massive, the academic pressure unrelenting. I loved every moment of it.

But I loved the people and the milieu even more. Union was a caring community. Everybody seemed to matter to everybody else. One day a few other students and I might be drinking beer with the great philosopher and theologian Reinhold Niebuhr, another day a couple of us would be teaching each other our techniques for remembering who did what to whom in

Deuteronomy, Second Kings, and Jeremiah, or embracing and holding somebody who needed to be comforted, or gathering around a grand piano on a
Sunday evening as we returned from our "field work" assignments in
churches around New York and New Jersey. In the Union community I was
left alone when I needed my private space, yet I was always surrounded by
friends whose acceptance, caring, and companionship renewed and strength-
ened my sense of self. My idea of an angry, judgemental, anthropomorphic
God disappeared completely, replaced by a sense of divine love. And the
questions of what initiated the Universe, and how, became irrelevant to my
daily life.

Not surprisingly, I stayed on at Union after my fellowship year was over.
The Master of Divinity degree was a three-year program. Although I had
gone to university to experience and to learn rather than to prepare myself
for a career, I began to contemplate my post-university future. I had already
decided against ordination and becoming a clergyman of some sort, and what
seemed to be emerging as a desirable possibility was to obtain the master's
degree and, after that, a doctorate in the philosophy of religion—with a view
to becoming a university teacher. But it was an idea for which I lacked any
great passion. And then, just when I was ready for it emotionally, the second
in the chain of events that was to alter the direction of my life occurred.

In order to finance the second and third years of my master's program, I
had accepted a position at Brooklyn Friends School, where I taught world
religions to high-school students two afternoons a week. Shortly after I began
teaching there, I met two other teachers who were keen amateur photographers. One day they invited me to accompany them to a special showing of
slides made by participants in a summer workshop they had attended, taught
by Helen Manzer. While both the visual and the technical qualities of the
photographs were superb, I was even more impressed by Helen, whose cri-
tique of the images was incredibly honest and direct, yet always helpful. Even
in this first meeting, I could tell that she was an unusual person in many
ways. In her late sixties, short and plump, she was wearing a plain khaki
shirt, a roomy khaki skirt, "sensible" brown walking shoes, and an Indian
headband, a rather unusual ensemble for 1960. This, I was to learn, was

what she always wore. Behind her thick glasses her eyes seemed always to be dancing, and her entire face lit up whenever she smiled, which was frequently. Clearly her students both respected and admired her. I signed up for an eight-night course.

The first night of the course Helen told each of her fifteen students to buy a specific Linhof tripod and a Leitz ball-and-socket head for the top of it, and to bring these to class the following week. Thirteen of us appeared with our equipment on the second night. When Helen inquired and found out that the other two had not yet made their purchases, she promptly returned their course fee and told them to leave. When they protested she replied, "If you're not serious, there's no place for you in this course," and she waited for them to go before saying another word. Needless to say, this put the fear of God into everybody else. And God she was, although I was no longer intimidated by the Almighty, just eager to learn everything I could.

Helen's course was about "making pictures," not taking them. She taught us how to use our cameras well, but, more important, she stressed learning to see, and using good visual design to convey on film what we were seeing. At long last somebody was consciously, actively satisfying my aesthetic appetite. I photographed everything around me, but even in the heart of New York City my primary interest was the natural world. I had begun to put the rose bush back into my garden.

After my first course with Helen (I would take two more with her), my thoughts of becoming a university teacher began to fade. I switched my major from philosophy of religion to practical theology, which enabled me to write my master's thesis on "still photography as a medium of religious expression" and to prepare an accompanying slides-with-music program. Although the thesis was illustrated with photographs made by several other photographers, it was nevertheless a highly academic document. The audiovisual presentation, on the other hand, was anything but academic. Using the music of Handel and Vivaldi and my own nature photographs, I celebrated the liberation of my spirit.

And then I graduated. With my particular academic pattern and degrees, the best I could hope for was to secure a teaching position at a junior college

Sam W. Morris

Dr. Helen Manzer, New York, who inspired me with her seeing and her teaching.

or a private educational institution, probably one affiliated with a religious denomination. In a somewhat scatter-shot fashion, I mailed off my curriculum vitae to a number of schools, then hitched a ride to California, crossing the continent for the first time. I had no idea what I was going to do when I arrived in California. I was twenty-four years old, and it didn't matter.

A high-school friend who was living in Sacramento provided me with some contacts, and I was hired for a month by Procter & Gamble to shovel cake mix into barrels and drop hand towels into boxes of detergent as they came by me on a conveyor belt. This put a little money in my pocket and gave me lots of time to think. After that I spent a couple of weeks hiking in the Sierras as one of four chaperone-guides for a group of teenagers from a Baptist church. This cost me nothing and gave me time to make pictures.

During the summer I was offered a teaching position in religious education at Alberta College, a United Church of Canada school in Edmonton. Since it was the only job offer I received, I accepted. I liked the idea of staying in the West. The mountains of California had revived my love of wild places, and I saw on a map that Edmonton was an easy drive away from the Rockies. So, one day in early September 1962, I boarded a bus in Sacramento and headed north. When I arrived in Edmonton, the gentleman from the college who met me could barely conceal his shock when the new religious-education teacher descended from the bus wearing faded Levis, scuffed cowboy boots, and a battered straw stetson. Apparently, I was not at all what he had in mind.

I was never entirely comfortable at Alberta College, despite the fact that I was given a great deal of freedom to establish courses and course content; the administration often seemed somewhat uneasy about me. At issue was the meaning of religious education. The principal and some others expected me to teach Christian education, but to me this was too narrow an approach. How was it possible to discuss Christianity intelligently without providing a solid background in the evolution of Jewish thought and culture? And wouldn't students benefit by learning about other major world religions? If nothing else, I thought, this would provide them with useful perspectives for evaluating their own religious experiences. In any event I was regarded,

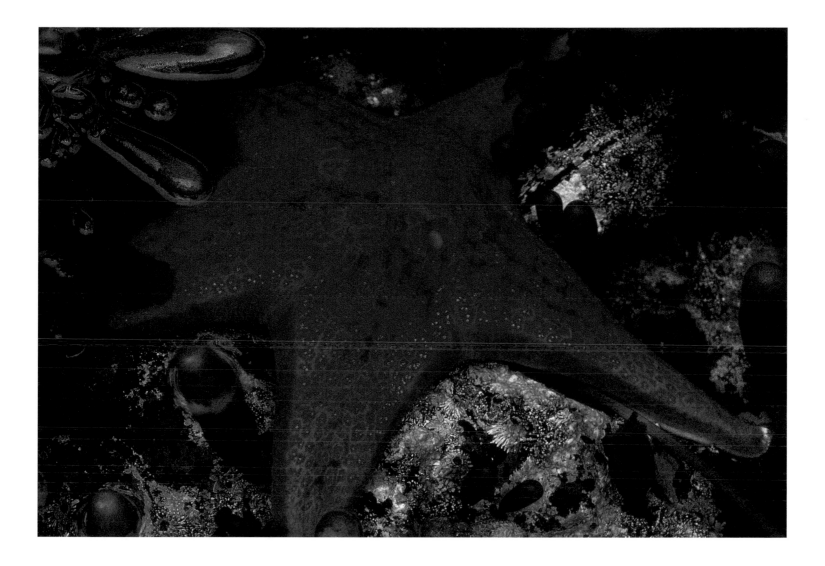

While living in Western Canada, I frequently photographed wildlife subjects—from elk to starfish—and found that careful attention to design invariably aided my efforts to provide clear, accurate documentation. However, I quickly realized that effective portrayal of a creature closeup, while often difficult technically, is often easier to achieve visually than a picture that emphasizes the creature's habitat. So, in this Pacific coast tide pool, as in many other situations, I made overall to close-up images in order to provide a range of perspectives.

not inaccurately I suppose, as a rather dubious Christian. Besides, I had grown a beard, which upset a number of parents. But to the administration's credit, they rarely tried to interfere with a program once it was established—even when I set up Alberta's first course in sex education, which many students needed and wanted.

My first year at Alberta College answered a lingering question for me. I realized that, while I loved teaching, especially interacting with students, I would never be completely happy in a career that was centred primarily on the communication of ideas. Due in large part to my childhood and adolescent experiences, both positive and negative, I wanted a creative milieu in which I could also express the sensual side of my nature and in which feelings could be openly acknowledged. In a word, what I wanted was balance.

While living in Edmonton, I became more involved in photography than ever. I was making pictures before rushing off to morning classes and again in the late afternoon and evening, mostly around the city. On weekends I was photographing in the mountains and foothills, in the badlands of southern Alberta, on the prairies—pictures of wild animals, plants, cloud formations, glaciers, rivers, ranch buildings, oil refineries, junkyards, motorcycle races, and rodeos. My list of subjects and my library of photographs were continually expanding, and my excitement with the medium was developing into a passion. I met many other amateur photographers throughout Alberta, some of whom were extremely keen and have become lifelong friends.

Provided a photographer has a good basic grounding in camera operation and visual design, he or she will learn most by making pictures regularly. There's really no substitute for this. Certainly, because of my motivation, my learning curve at this point was climbing rapidly. Also, I was well aware of the learning value teaching had for a teacher. So with motives that included self-interest, I made arrangements with the Edmonton YWCA to offer an evening course in photography, patterned after those I had taken with Helen Manzer. Four amateur photographers enrolled. I was not, after all, a household name in Edmonton or anywhere else.

The students learned and so did I. We enjoyed discussing one another's images, and we enjoyed one another so much as people that, during the thirty years since, I have rarely visited Edmonton without seeing all or most of the four. The second time I offered the course, sixteen people enrolled, including the original four, and the third time the Y had to cut off registration at thirty-five.

About the same time as my photographic activities were expanding rapidly in Edmonton, they were also growing in Toronto. Through one of Helen's summer students, I had heard of and joined the Toronto Guild for Colour Photography, a large camera club that had a busy schedule of programs and activities, including clinics for evaluation of photographs and competitions that I could enter by mail. The feedback I received was invaluable to me, and served to intensify my fervour.

By now my life revolved around photography. It was only a matter of time before I would give up teaching religion, philosophy, and sex education. I began haunting magazine stores and the public library, examining dozens of publications in hope of finding some that might be interested in using my pictures. I carefully prepared and mailed submissions of photographs to one magazine after another. Finally, on my nineteenth or twentieth attempt, I scored. *Weekend* magazine, carried on Saturdays by a number of major Canadian daily newspapers, purchased a winter-twilight picture of rush-hour traffic in Edmonton for its "This Is Canada" series. The photograph appeared in December 1964, nearly a year after my sale. I was so overwhelmed with excitement that I bought twenty copies of the magazine, and I still have several of them tucked away in a drawer.

Not long after this initial success, I sold three picture stories, each with an accompanying article, to *Weekend*'s rival, *The Star Weekly*, in rather quick succession. The first of these—about the psychology involved in getting close to wild animals in order to photograph them—drew on my childhood experiences of working with animals on the farm. When it appeared under the title "How to Win Wild Friends and Influence Animals," I was somewhat chagrined. Dale Carnegie, Norman Vincent Peale, and their ilk were not my philosophical soulmates.

Other magazines were also buying photographs from me, even though I was still receiving more rejection slips than purchase orders. However, when

I tallied my photographic income against my expenses at the end of 1964, I discovered that I had earned as much from the sale of my pictures during the year as I had spent on film, processing, and gasoline. So I resigned my position at Alberta College, effective the following June. It was madness, I suppose, since my worldly goods at the time consisted of a used Volkswagen Beetle, two cameras, two lenses, a tripod, and $800 in cash. But after living from hand to mouth for most of my seven years of university and surviving, I had no hang-ups about financial security. Being very poor, if necessary, would not be a new experience for me. However, just before the school year ended, I was hired by Berkeley Studio, the United Church of Canada still- and motion-picture production house in Toronto.

Berkeley kept me in the West for several months, primarily to photograph church homes for senior citizens in Alberta and British Columbia, so I continued to make Edmonton my home until February 1966. And while I was still living there, an event occurred that propelled me faster and farther along my new career path than I had dared to dream possible.

One October day the owner of an Edmonton film-processing lab passed me an opened envelope addressed to the lab containing a note and another envelope. The note read simply, "If Freeman Patterson should ever come into your lab, please give him the enclosed envelope," and was signed: Lorraine Monk, Executive Producer, Still Photography Division, National Film Board of Canada. (I was later to learn that Lorraine had sent identical packages to more than twenty other film-processing labs across the country in hope of tracking me down.)

I hardly dared to open the envelope. I knew it couldn't be bad news, but how could it be good news? Since I'd never heard of Lorraine Monk and she didn't know me, why was she writing to me? I could tell that there was a long letter inside, and while one part of me wanted to know what it said, another part was apprehensive, afraid that it would be nothing of importance.

In the letter Lorraine explained that the film board had been commissioned by the federal government to produce two books for Canada's centennial year—a book of black-and-white images of Canadian people, and a much larger book containing 260 colour images of the Canadian landscape from coast to coast in all four seasons. She wrote that she was looking for already-existing photographs for the second book and also for photographers who could shoot on assignment in various parts of Canada at specific times of the year. She went on to say that she had seen one of my colour images reproduced as a small black-and-white in an American magazine and, on the strength of that image and the little bit that was written about me, she would like me to submit about 100 photographs for her consideration.

Returning to my apartment, I immediately set to work going through all my Canadian landscape and nature pictures. My editing was brutal, the toughest I'd ever been on my own work. A few days later I committed the best of my work and my dreams to the not-always-dependable hands of Canada Post. Before the package even had time to arrive, it seemed, I received a telephone call from Lorraine's assistant, who reported that Lorraine liked the photographs and wanted to see an even larger selection. This time I loosened up a little in my editing. I had to. I'd already sent off what I considered my finest images.

After I mailed the second package, there was only silence, and before long my insides were churning. I began to alternate between hoping that the delay meant the film board was going to keep some slides and fearing that I had ruined my chances with my second submission. I even worried that my registered package had been lost in the mail. Fortunately I had work to do in British Columbia for Berkeley Studio, something to prevent the suspense from debilitating me utterly. Before I left Edmonton I took the precaution of sending a note to Lorraine's assistant, giving him addresses and phone numbers just in case he needed to contact me.

The telephone wakened me very early one morning in my Vancouver hotel room, and an unfamiliar voice asked me to hold. Lorraine Monk wanted to speak with me. When she came on the line, the first thing she said was, "What time is it there? I've just remembered this country has several time zones." After I told her that it was only 5:30, but I really didn't mind, she breezed on, "Oh well, in that case . . ." and proceeded to tell me that she wanted to buy seventy of my photographs. How did $7,000 sound? And was I available to do some assignment shooting for the book while I was still in the West? At $100 per day, plus film and expenses.

My contact with the film board immediately took precedence in my mind over my employment by Berkeley Studio. For one thing, film-board assignments such as "the prairies in winter" and "Manitoba in spring" held out the prospect of travelling and of making the sort of images that mattered most to me. For another, the years of working on the farm and teaching at Alberta College had made me realize how much I disliked being locked into a schedule.

In February I set out for Toronto. Having shipped what little furniture I owned, I stuffed everything else into the Beetle and drove slowly and circuitously across Saskatchewan and Manitoba, photographing the prairies in winter for the film board's book on Canada. At long last I was doing what I wanted to do and getting paid for it.

The exact chronology of events that formed my life for the seven years that I lived in Toronto has largely faded from my memory, I suppose because I became involved with so many people and so many interconnecting projects and activities. But although the chronology is dim, key experiences are not, and in retrospect I can probably connect them up more clearly than I ever could have done at the time.

As soon as I arrived, I became a full member of the Toronto Guild for Colour Photography and met many fine amateur photographers whom I had known only by reputation. All of them were wonderfully friendly and helpful, and through them I soon became part of a large network of amateurs in the city and its surrounding communities, which in turn led to contacts and friendships across Canada and the United States. Many of the Toronto photographers were highly accomplished in various aspects of nature photography, such as wildflowers and birds, and extremely generous in sharing their knowledge of both photography and natural history. I soaked up information faster than I could possibly put it to actual use, and was excited by my association with so many people for whom making pictures was a major creative outlet. To this day I remain convinced that the majority of Canada's finest photographers are amateurs, and that in the basements, dens, and darkrooms of the nation there exists an undiscovered treasure trove of superb photographic images documenting, above all else, our better selves.

On the other hand, I came to realize that many amateurs lacked a comprehensive knowledge of visual design and, as a result, tended to rely on simple formulas derived from established principles in composing their images. While I respected their dedicated efforts, I was often less happy with their critiques of other photographers' work, especially when they were in a position to influence the creative development of beginners. I also observed that the photographers who were most willing to experiment visually were usually those who were most comfortable with themselves as persons.

My association with amateurs, especially in Toronto, strongly influenced the direction and development of my career, especially over the next ten or fifteen years. It led to my decision to establish the summer workshops that I've conducted in New Brunswick since 1973 and in South Africa since 1984. First in Edmonton and then in Toronto, I became increasingly aware of what photographers were looking for by way of instruction, and realized over time that I could offer them something of value. I also perceived the areas that photographers were not exploring but, in my opinion, should have been. For example, the building blocks of language (nouns, verbs, adjectives, etc.) and their arrangement in phrases, sentences, and paragraphs seemed directly parallel with the building blocks of visual design (shapes, lines, textures, etc.) and their arrangement in picture space, and I gradually incorporated these subjects into my teaching. The workshops, in turn, led to my writing four instructional books on photography and visual design, which in their turn have contributed substantially to the development of other books and projects. Since the collective contribution of amateur photographers to my life and career has been so great, I doubt that more than a very few realize the value of their own individual contributions or the depth of my gratitude.

My stay at Berkeley Studio lasted just over a year, during which time I also completed two or three more assignments for the Still Photography Division of the National Film Board. Late in May 1967, after first touring the wonders of Expo 67, the World's Fair in Montreal, I flew to South Africa and on to Botswana, which had become an independent nation less than six months earlier. My sister and brother-in-law were spending a year there as volunteer teachers in Serowe, the old tribal capital, which was a collection of thousands of *rondawels* (round mud huts with thatched roofs) spread over an arid, hilly plain. After the pilot had swooped low enough to scatter a herd of goats grazing on the landing-strip, he brought the ageing DC-3 down in a cloud of dust, disgorging me onto the African veld along with four cardboard cartons of day-old chicks that had been occupying the seat behind me. Less than forty-eight hours had passed since I had left Toronto, but in many respects I had journeyed centuries backward in time. I had no way of knowing at that moment that my long-time love affair with southern Africa had begun, and that one day people would refer to me as "the Afri-Canadian," or even more particularly as "the Namaqua-Canadian," because of my many long visits to Namaqualand in the northwest corner of South Africa.

After spending about three weeks with my sister and brother-in-law, I set off on a six-week tour of the Botswana bushveld, hitching rides in four-by-four pick-up trucks driven by Peace Corps volunteers, medical officers, or other government employees. We carried most of our food and all of our water and petrol with us, and spent most nights camping under a canopy of stars far more numerous and infinitely brighter than I had ever experienced in North America, or walking in the brilliant light of a full moon that turned granules of sand into glittering diamonds. During the days we snaked through the bush along dry dirt tracks that frequently deteriorated into pure sand and mired the vehicle for hours. Here and there we came across tiny, remote villages where ageing veterans of the Second World War, or their widows, or others waited by the dusty track (for weeks, sometimes) for their annual pension of about five dollars or for a visit from a medical officer. At many stops the excited ululating and dancing of village women greeted our arrival, and everywhere we were received warmly and with natural graciousness.

I left Botswana in the middle of August, having made at least 8,000 photographs, and crossed the border into South Africa, in many respects a

Man drinking tea in his family *rondawel* near Francistown, Botswana, on my first visit to Africa, 1967.

very different country then from what it is today. Linking up with a photographer from the South Africa Tourist Corporation, who turned out to be delightfully iconoclastic and totally out of synch with his nation's politics, I had a not-your-typical-tourist trip around the eastern half of the country, then hopped a bus in Durban and rode it all the way to Cape Town and back again, making a few stops along the way. The topography of South Africa is so varied and so compellingly beautiful that by the time I arrived back in Durban I discovered that I had exposed another 4,000 photographs. Also, I had plenty of opportunities to witness and to experience some of the profound differences between life under South Africa's apartheid system and life in the new democracy of Botswana.

Two or three days after returning to Durban, I had a sudden urge to go home. The emotional trigger might have been a brief, but heavy rain shower, the first rain I'd experienced since leaving Canada. I recall leaning far out of my hotel window until my head and shoulders were streaming with water.

A few days later, in the middle of September, I flew into Montreal, where those of us who were continuing on to Toronto also had to disembark in order to clear immigration and customs. Even though I was sure that a copy of *Canada: A Year of the Land*, the National Film Board's centennial book, would be waiting for me at home, I dashed upstairs to a bookstore and bought a copy. Wedged between two obviously uninterested businessmen, I passed the hour's flight to Toronto turning the pages of the largest and most beautiful book of photographs ever produced in Canada up to that time, and lingering over portions of Bruce Hutchison's accompanying text. While I had known that several of my images would be included in the book, I was not emotionally prepared for the discovery that 55 of the 260 photographs were mine. As the plane landed in Toronto, I was flying higher than I had ever flown before. At $25 (a huge price in those days), the book sold over a million copies, in large part because "ordinary" Canadians loved it. I remember the day that my mailman knocked on my door to enquire if I were the Freeman Patterson who had all those photos in the big new book he had just bought for his wife, and another day when a small-airplane pilot in St. Hubert,

Lorraine Monk, Executive Director, Still Photography Division, National Film Board of Canada, presenting me with a copy of the 1967 centennial book *Canada: A Year of the Land*, which contained many of my photographs.

Quebec, told me that he had purchased a copy for his family of eight children. I celebrated Canada's 100th birthday more personally and more euphorically than I could ever have anticipated.

Just because I had suddenly become fairly well known as a photographer did not mean that I was immediately deluged with professional assignments. In fact, work was not all that plentiful in the year following our birthday bash—the first year that I operated entirely as a freelance photographer— probably because nobody had any money left. However, I managed to survive on a small amount of shooting for advertising agencies, by continuing to sell photographs to magazines for editorial use, and by commencing an association with a stock-photography agency. The sizeable library of good pictures I had built up over the years proved to be my financial salvation.

However, at the beginning of 1968, I was as poor as I'd ever been. Having spent virtually all of my savings on my trip to Africa (particularly on buying film for the trip), I needed cash. In a way, it was amateur photographers who rescued me, although they were unaware of my financial circumstances. At the urging and under the sponsorship of the Toronto Guild, the club to which I belonged, I used my slides of Botswana and South Africa to produce my first major audio-visual program, a two-hour show of slides-with-voice-and-music. "Two Faces of Africa" played for two nights to capacity houses at Toronto's Eaton Auditorium, and took my mind off bread and butter. During the year the show was sponsored in five other major Canadian cities, which put more money in my pocket and resulted in my second trip to Africa.

Unbeknown to me, some members of the South African embassy had attended my Ottawa presentation, and several weeks later a senior officer contacted me. Commenting on my show, he remarked, "You were objective. You didn't butter us up, and you didn't criticize us unfairly." Then he asked me if I would like to make a second visit to South Africa, "as a guest of the government, but with absolutely no strings attached." I was stunned by the offer, but not overwhelmed. I had to consider what benefits the embassy expected to derive from my visit, whether or not I could maintain my objectivity, and in what ways the trip could be useful to me. We discussed a two-month itinerary, and I was pleased to find that no location I wanted to visit was considered "off limits," including Soweto. I'm probably not colour-blind, but I think I'm about as close to it as a human being can get, and I had no desire to paint South Africa white—or, for that matter, black. So, early in October 1969, back to South Africa I went. (I also revisited Botswana briefly at my own expense.)

During the trip another event, a tiny one, occurred that was to influence the course of my career and my life profoundly. One day in Johannesburg, just before I returned home, I happened to notice an advertisement for a photographic exhibition, sponsored by the Photographic Society of Southern Africa, which was to take place in the city that very night. After viewing the prints and watching an excellent slide show, I made the acquaintance of a number of photographers, again mostly amateurs. We subsequently kept in touch, and in 1976 I was invited back to South Africa to give three days of lectures and audiovisual programs at the society's annual congress. After seeing my nature photographs, several photographers encouraged me to visit Namaqualand, in the northwest corner of the country, a remote region famed for the most spectacular annual spring display of wildflowers on the planet. (I tucked this information away and, when I was invited back to South Africa in 1980, I made plans to visit this remarkable place.)

I returned to Toronto just before Christmas 1969 with another 10,000 photographs, but before I even had the opportunity to sort and file them I received a call from a would-be tour operator in New York City, asking if I would be interested in being the "official photographer" for an educational safari and tour of East Africa (Kenya, Tanzania, and Uganda) that was departing in mid-February—no professional fee, but all travel costs paid. I accepted and, in no time, it seemed, I was back in Africa.

However, I was also travelling in Canada. I toured around Ontario every spring and autumn, spent the summers of 1968 and 1969 in Alberta and British Columbia, and made trips to New Brunswick to visit my parents. Wherever I went, I photographed, and my library of slides continued to grow. By 1970 my pictures were selling regularly to advertising agencies, magazines, and other clients, and I was receiving an increasing number of

With a group of Inuit boys at Holman, when I was travelling as a member of the press party with Governor General Roland Michener and Mrs. Michener during their 1970 tour of the western Arctic.

assignments from corporations such as the St. Lawrence Seaway Authority and Reader's Digest Books. Also, more and more amateur photographic groups were asking me for instructional slide lectures, and I usually accepted for the price of my gas or simply as a way of repaying in kind photographers who had been (and still were) so helpful to me. But, as my activities increased, I found myself becoming more and more of a clerk. The purely practical side of my business—sorting, editing, numbering, filing, and delivering photographs; keeping records; and so on—consumed a great deal of my time and bored me silly.

In 1971, for the first time in many years, I went home for Christmas, and invited my friend Dennis Mills, a freelance editor with a good knowledge of visual design, to come along with me. On New Year's Day 1972 we climbed the hill on Shamper's Bluff to the field where my house now stands. At the time the property (about seventy hectares) was owned jointly by my father and my aunt. It was a place I knew well, having worked here as a teenager with my father for several summers, helping the owners at the time to "bring in the hay" in return for their helping us to bring in ours. Parts of the hilltop meadow had grown up in alder bushes, but we still had a clear view of the fields below, of the broad expanse of water where the Belleisle River flows into the St. John River, and the hills beyond—one of the loveliest panoramas in southern New Brunswick. "Here," I told Dennis, "is where I want to have workshops."

Before we walked down the hill to the Shamper's Bluff road, Dennis and I had examined the view from every part of the field, chosen a site for a building, and decided on its orientation. He was as keen about my idea as I was. So I put the proposal to my father, who, I knew, would not be against it as long as I could foresee a profit; then Dennis and I drove back to Toronto, brainstorming about building plans and workshop plans the entire way.

Moving from Toronto in the summer of 1972, we began construction immediately, continued through the fall and winter, and had the house (with its basement workshop area) virtually completed by spring, but it would never have happened without the support and work of my family, including my father, and the contributions of many friends and neighbours. On the calm, sunny evening of June 3, 1973, one and a half years after Dennis and I had climbed the hill at Shamper's Bluff, we celebrated the beginning of the first workshop. My mother planted a maple tree, Lorraine Monk planted another, my photographer friend Jessie Mackenzie planted a third, and our neighbour Vera Shamper planted a fourth. Several of the people at the party and many of those registered for the first workshop were members of the Toronto Guild for Colour Photography.

I can lie in the shade of the maple trees now, or photograph the shadow pattern of their branches streaming across the snow. And, beyond them, I can see my barn snuggled against the forest and a small second house where my aunt Helen lives for several months of the year.

For more than twenty years, Shamper's Bluff has been home, not because I live and work here much of the year, but because I am part of a nourishing, enabling, sustaining community, including humans, from which I take and to which I give.

In 1979, I photographed Zaidee Williams of Long Reach in her Loyalist finery, which was typical of that worn by the ancestors of many people in the lower St. John River valley.

CONTINENT
OF LIGHT

THERE WAS A TIME WHEN EARTH HAD NO EYES—A VERY LONG TIME INDEED.
Only since about 600 million years ago, or for the last 4 per cent of its life,
has Earth been able to see. With our superb eyesight and with instruments
that now extend the range of human vision far into the macrocosm of the
universe and into the microcosm of a cell, we have difficulty conceiving of the
turbulent, gaseous planet cooling to form a crust, oceans forming, continents
separating and sailing about, and plants coming ashore and colonizing the
land masses, without any of the action being observed. When eyes eventually
evolved, millions more years passed by before there were creatures with vision
good enough for us to call it "seeing." And yet, the planet had always been
bathed by the light of our sun.

In the very recent past, it was common to speak of "darkest Africa." The
use of the term always seemed to imply two things: that much of the continent was unexplored, and therefore unseen (by people who did not live there,
of course), and that it was primitive, again unseen (a continent held in the
sway of the unconscious, incapable of being understood, a place beneath
vision). Even now this most magnificent of continents is seen only superfi-
cially by the millions of tourists who come to spend a few exciting days or
weeks "on safari," because packaging Africa is like trying to package one's
soul. Here, where human life began, one encounters mysteries that, if
acknowledged, twist and bend our perceptions of who and what we really are.
The intellect, reason, and logic, so revered in Western cultures, often seem
thoroughly foreign to the continent's deserts, savannahs, rain forests, and

Quiver trees (kokerbome) at sunrise, Richtersveld National Park, South Africa.

even its huge, modern cities and, more than anywhere else I've ever been, inadequate to grasp messages from "that part of the psyche which retains and transmits the common psychological inheritance of mankind," which Carl Jung called "the collective unconscious." The amount of time I have spent in Africa can now be counted in years. I have fallen under its spell, and it's everything that I feel about Africa, not what I understand, that draws me back again and again.

Every time the plane from North America begins to parallel the coast of Namibia, I look out the window and watch the slow-motion approach of the thin white line of surf that separates the cold, steel-blue wilderness of water from the hot, coppery-beige wilderness of sand, and I experience the sensation of being a visitor from space witnessing for the very first time the architectural grandeur of a strange planet.

And then, I am over Africa.

Far, far below me, erosion patterns of 10,000 centuries form dark threads in the unending carpet of sand, the wind constantly altering and shifting the designs of the spaces between the permanent stitches. For a while no tracery of roads, no marks of human habitation mar my experience of seeing the planet before the time of eyes.

The deserts of southern Africa are no less impressive from the ground. Their names resonate in the ear and in the imagination—"the sands of the Kalahari," "Bushmanland," "the Great Sand Sea of Namibia." Sunrise transforms Earth everywhere, but nowhere is the transformation more complete than in the enormous dunes of the Great Sand Sea, and nowhere else have I been so aware that the rising sun makes no sound. Silence is soul music.

However, I have another sort of music to hear, and another story to tell. It is the story of flowers—how tales of their beauty lured me to the Namib's southerly extreme, Namaqualand, which lies across the Orange River, in the northwest corner of South Africa, and how in searching for the flowers I discovered a second home. Like meeting Helen Manzer while I was studying in New York and receiving the letter from Lorraine Monk while I was teaching and photographing in Edmonton—both events that changed the course and direction of my life—what happened on my first visit to Namaqualand can be described, on the one hand, as pure chance and, on the other hand, as pure grace.

In the middle of September 1980 (late spring), a friend and I flew from Johannesburg to the town of Upington in the north-central part of South Africa. From there we headed west on horrendous dirt roads towards Namaqualand on the Atlantic coast, a semi-arid and desert region of lowveld (typically, rolling dunes covered sparsely with low shrubs and grasses) and mountainous highveld that contains some of the planet's greatest boulders and rockscapes. Finally, I hoped, I would see "the flowers" South African friends had told me about, but I couldn't be sure. None of my friends in the big cities had been able to tell me whether or not I would be on time for the annual display and had only vague suggestions about whom to contact for information once I arrived. Since none of them had ever visited Namaqualand and they had only seen photographs of the region in spring, I suppose I could hardly have expected anything else.

We stopped the first night at the little *dorp* (village) of Pofadder, and I thought, both because of its remote location and because of its being named after a snake, that I had reached the end of Earth. The next day we pressed on across the Bushmanland desert towards the little mining town of Aggeneys, often forced by deep ruts in the sand or rocky soil to move slowly through what seemed like endless veld.

The following morning we continued westward across the desert towards Springbok, but soon stopped to walk across flat or rolling stretches of red sand that were dotted here and there with the skeletons of shrubs and interrupted in the distance by low buttes or pyramid-like mountains. I know now that some years this lonely panorama is blanketed with flowers, but that day its sheer emptiness attracted us.

Just after we resumed our journey, we encountered our first flowers—an occasional white mesembryanthemum and, in a shallow depression of cracked mud, a few brilliant yellow gazanias. Then, within a kilometre, the earth was transformed. Yellow gazanias stretched across the red sand as far as our eyes could see—a startling contrast to the inverted blue bowl of the sky. But there was none of the famous Bushmanland daisies, or the incredible tapestry of species and colours that, in the years since, have so often left me in a state of speechless wonder.

After a day of exploring and making pictures around the town of Springbok, it became evident to my friend and me that the flower season had peaked weeks earlier, so the next morning we headed south on the main highway, pausing now and then to photograph a colourful bush or clump of flowers lingering among the rocks. About noon we passed the village of Kamieskroon and turned west on a side road towards the ocean. Here and there small pools of water in ditches reflected remnants of the flower season, and I remember finding a patch of flowers that was past its prime, but still so filled with a variety of colours that for the last two hours of daylight I crawled about on my knees or lay on my stomach, recording the mix of hues and creating colour abstracts. Then, because we had no accommodation for the night, we backtracked to Kamieskroon, having noticed a "Hotel" sign at the entrance to the village when we passed by earlier in the day. Fortunately for us, the last of the nine rooms was available.

While we were eating dinner in the little dining-room, the hotel owner–manager, Colla Swart, told the other guests (who were travelling in a group and whom she seemed to know) that she would show them some of her flower slides right after the meal. Since my friend and I were keen to see some pictures of Namaqualand in bloom and had nothing else to do, we asked if we might stay for the slide show.

Colla set up her projector on an empty table and, as she shone the first slide on the wall, announced in rapid-fire Afrikaans (with a few words of English thrown in for my benefit) that this was the first time in her life that she had shown her pictures to anybody other than her family. "Just as well," I thought after viewing a few more of the slides, most of which showed a vast expanse of blue sky with a few people or goats strolling through some flowers scattered among the village buildings. To make matters worse, half of the pictures were seriously overexposed because, as Colla explained repeatedly, her new telephoto lens didn't work properly. Or, something else had gone wrong. Her running commentary was a litany of apologies.

Just about the time I was beginning to regret ever having asked to stay for her show, Colla started to project slides that showed flowers carpeting the veld. Some fields were all of one colour, others an intricate tapestry of hues. She showed masses of flowers sweeping among boulders, or tumbling down mountainsides, or stretching in a long, broad line down the middle of a dirt road. The composition and technical quality of the images were still god-awful, but the subject matter was incredible. Clearly, all the stories that my friends in Johannesburg and Pretoria had told me about the flowers of Namaqualand were true. I was beside myself with excitement, on the one hand, and, on the other, disappointed beyond measure that I had missed this year's display. But even then, I knew I would be coming back.

While Colla was packing up her projector and talking to the other guests, I slipped back to my room and dug a copy of *Photography and the Art of Seeing*, my second instructional photography book, out of my suitcase. Returning to the dining-room, I thanked Colla for her show and gave her the book, explaining that it should help her to overcome some of her photographic problems. However, I did not tell her that I was the author.

The next morning, while I was eating scrambled eggs and smoked kippers, Colla charged into the dining-room and over to my table. "I have a bone to pick with you," she announced in suddenly fluent English. Somewhat alarmed, I asked what I had done to offend. "You're a professional photographer," she replied. "You sat through my slide show last night without telling me, and I am mortified!" When I asked how she knew I was a professional, she told me that she had started to read the book in bed, and when the lights went out (in those days the hotel generator was turned off every night at 10:00) she got a flashlight and continued reading until about 3:00, when it suddenly occurred to her that the author's name on the front of the book was the same name I had signed in the hotel register.

But if Colla had startled me with her initial approach, she surprised me even more with what she said next. "If you can stay for a couple of days, I'll cancel everything I have to do"—in addition to running the hotel, she managed a hostel for 150 neglected children of colour, taught English two hours a day in the village school, and was supervising the building of some senior citizens' apartments for the local Dutch Reformed Church—and I'll show you the best flowers we have left in Namaqualand this year, provided you'll teach me everything you can about photography."

I stayed. And so began my long relationship with Colla, her family, and Namaqualand, an experience that continues to shape and bless my life. In the years since our initial meeting, Kamieskroon has become my second home, and the Swarts my second family. But it didn't happen all at once.

After breakfast that first morning, we set off up the mountain pass behind the hotel—normally a twenty-minute drive—as the flowers on the mountain plateaus always bloom last. Two hours later we had not reached the top, as I was continually shouting, "Stop, stop!" Years later Colla admitted to me that, long before we had reached the top of the pass, she had said to herself, "This man is crazy!" Usually she put a roll of film in her camera every Christmas, and took it out the following Christmas, whereas I had gone through four rolls in less than two hours. Fully aware by now of how excited I was by the flowers, she started driving at break-neck speed from one spectacular display to the next. Somehow I managed to get through the day without complaining too much, but the next morning I asked her to choose two locations only—one for the morning and one for the afternoon—so I could make photographs carefully and also give her some good basic instruction.

Despite the fact that I wanted to stay longer, my friend and I had to leave the following morning. As we climbed into our vehicle and waved goodbye, Colla promised to let me know if the flowers were good next year.

On September 1 the following year, I was reading a newpaper in my kitchen when the telephone rang. The telegraph office had a message for me from South Africa: "Flowers excellent. Come at once. Colla Swart." Nine days later I was winging north from Cape Town along the Atlantic coast in a tiny plane, dazed by the expanse and profusion of colour below. I stayed that night in a hotel in Springbok.

Colla arrived the next morning at 7:00, and we set out in her *bakkie* (pick-up truck). The farther we drove, the more spectacular the flowers along the roadside seem to become. Finally, I asked Colla to stop, and clambered up over one of the banks. On the other side waves of flowers rolled into a multicoloured sea. Six hours later I had exposed sixteen rolls of film and, in the process, given Colla more lessons on the use of her camera and lenses.

It was probably on that day that I first began to perceive how different Colla's way of thinking was from mine. When I had first met her a year earlier, I gleaned the impression that she was somewhat scatterbrained. Now, I realized how terribly wrong I had been. She was obviously an extremely intelligent person, but her intelligence was manifested in considerable part by an unusual ability to think and act laterally, to do many quite different things more or less simultaneously. It soon occurred to me that Colla naturally operated as if life were a web, and that she had to attend to all the strands at once. How else could she successfully manage a hotel and a hostel for neglected children, teach English, supervise the construction of church apartments, and attend to a host of other community and family matters, all at the same time? On the other hand, while it is also typical of me to be working on several major projects simultaneously, mine tend to be more obviously related to one another than Colla's do, and I usually proceed on each project in a logical, step-by-step fashion.

I also observed that, while I like orderliness, Colla seemed to operate most effectively when surrounded by clutter—which she often created naturally. When everything was on the table, she could see what she had to deal with. Or, to give her moral interpretation, "I want to be fair to everybody and everything."

During the next several years Colla and I had no end of struggles—sometimes battles—over our respective methodologies, as well as grave misunderstandings caused by our respective colloquial English. However, both of us steadfastly refused to let these differences wreck our developing friendship. We discovered early on that there is great therapeutic value in a good bottle of Cabernet Sauvignon and a willingness to talk, and have reached a place where our silences are as pregnant with understanding and caring as our times of laughter.

By 1983 Colla's visual skills and ability to handle a camera had developed significantly. That year she and her husband, Coenie, spent five weeks with me in Canada, and during their stay attended one of my New Brunswick workshops. I had already raised with them the possibility of having work-shops at the Kamieskroon Hotel during the flower season, so the visit answered many of their questions. Although they wondered who might come, they were aware that I had made major presentations to South African photographers in the past and, as a result, was quite well known. Besides, there were the flowers.

We advertised two workshops for 1984, which turned out to be the poor-est year for flowers in decades. The first workshop drew a grand total of three students, one from the United States, and registration for the second workshop was only marginally larger. But neither Colla nor I was discour-aged in the least. Instead, we exclaimed how fortunate we were that so few people had signed up in this obviously unusual year. And it really was a bless-ing in disguise, because it forced us to examine our visual preconceptions—to turn our eyes and our cameras to subjects other than flowers.

As spectacular as the spring display of flowers can be and usually is, flowers are only one fleeting aspect of Namaqualand's topography and com-plex ecosystems. Birds, insects, reptiles, and small mammals abound. There are gigantic lichen-covered rocks, rippling rock faces sculpted by eons of wind and water erosion, sand-dunes on the lowveld, and Atlantic breakers that soar twenty metres into the air as they crash against the rocky coast. There are unusual cloud formations, violent electrical storms, and glowing sunsets that bronze the landscape. And there are people, especially indigenous people, all of whom Colla seems to know and love and who love her.

By 1995 the number of workshops had expanded to eight, including the autumn months of March, April, and May, as well as the spring months of August and September, and some of the workshops (limited to fifteen or sixteen persons each) had long waiting lists. A third instructor, J.J. van Heerden, from Cape Town, had become part of our team four years earlier. While Colla participates in every workshop, J.J. and I either take turns or, as sometimes happens, come at the same time to make a teaching team of three.

The Namaqualand workshops have a sense of community about them, and often a feeling of communion. There are a number of reasons for this. First, there is the remarkable topography and natural history of

With my friend and teaching partner, photographer Colla Swart, at the Kamieskroon Hotel in Namaqualand, 1992.

Mel Gray

Namaqualand, and the relative remoteness of Kamieskroon from all major urban areas. There is the little Kamieskroon Hotel, now operated by Colla and Coenie's daughter and son-in-law. People from every walk and station of life meet and talk and laugh together on the front *stoep* or in the tiny bar, an oasis at the end of a long, hot day—bikers from Germany completing the last leg of a trans-Africa journey, social workers, a school inspector, a vanload of retirees from Cape Town, geologists, a family from Namibia, a television crew, and people from the village. I've often remarked that, if you stay long enough, you'll meet everybody from southern Africa—and half the rest of the world. And there are the workshop participants themselves, some of whom have returned many times, and who occupy much of the hotel space during their stay. While every group assumes its own special character or "colour" (azure, beige, scarlet), invariably there is a coming together that, time and again, lifts and renews my spirit. But to say that is utterly to understate the powerful spiritual impact the workshop communities have had on me and on my teaching.

I have long assumed that the fundamental reason anybody enrols in a workshop of any sort is to improve the quality of his or her life. Photography (dance, writing, hockey) is a passport, a means to achieving this greater end. So, while ostensibly people come to improve their visual and photographic skills, a good teacher not only will endeavour to help them learn what they want to know, but also will be cognizant of the deeper reasons for their being there. I recognized from the outset that Colla knew this in her bones, and that initially her main contribution to the workshops would be to be herself. Although, in the years since, Colla has so mastered the use of her tools, developed her powers of observation, and improved her ability to visualize effective compositions that these skills have become the servants of her imagination, it is still Colla the person who sets the stage for every workshop.

My role in the workshops is to provide form or structure. First, to make students aware of the designs behind the obvious labels of things: for example, to see a plate as a circular shape or, from a different position, as an oval or, from another position yet, as a straight line that is oriented vertically, horizontally, or obliquely. Then, to show them how the particular shape or line relates to other shapes and lines, especially within the closed space of a picture frame. In other words, I help participants to recognize existing patterns and to create new ones that express different ideas or evoke different feelings. If my presentation is clear, then in the process of learning about visual design, students will make the mental and emotional connections that enable them to recognize that the compositions of their photographs are metaphors or symbols for their own life patterns. As a result, many will consciously, and often aggressively, experiment with new visual designs as a way of creating and testing new patterns for their lives.

It is difficult to change our life patterns, even those we dislike the most. But the perception that a camera always looks in both directions and that visual design is a metaphor or symbol for life design is liberating. The accepting fellowship of a workshop community allows this perception to be acknowledged, talked about, mulled over. From there it is a very short step to talking about important personal experiences and sharing feelings. Often for the first time, it's all right to expose a deep wound or admit your insecurity. It's okay to cry. Nobody will think it at all strange if you hug someone of the same gender, or start dancing partway through dinner. In fact, they'll probably join you. But, if you just want to stick to picture-making, nobody will think the less of you.

When the artistic medium—in our case, photography—actually functions as a passport that enables people to enter new personal territory, the instructor of the workshop can benefit as much as the participants. On the final morning of a recent workshop, each participant presented a short slide essay—many of them personally revealing and deeply moving. After the last essay had been projected, everyone in the room seemed held in the grip of a holy hush. Eventually realizing that it was past time for lunch, I rose to speak a few words that would conclude the session, but what came out instead was, "I feel utterly surrounded by love." This connectedness—being touched by and in touch with others, and thereby with myself—is at the very heart of my Namaqualand experience.

However, something even more fundamental, more primal is involved. "Stone and sand and sea and sky" (the title of a song well known in Canada and Namaqualand) have shaped the lives of Namaqualanders, both physically and spiritually, for so long and to such a degree that it is impossible to understand the people well apart from their place. Coming from a region of rain and snow; of rivers, lakes, and marshes; of forests and farms, I was lured to Namaqualand by the promise of flowers, but quickly found myself establishing powerful emotional bonds to this arid, rock-strewn land. In fact, I felt that I was coming home, even though the only desert I had ever known was the local gravel pit, created by the provincial Department of Transportation.

Namaqualand is the southern end of a vast, topographically varied desert region that stretches north along the Atlantic Ocean from South Africa, through Namibia, into Angola. In living and travelling in this great desert, where landforms often are so stripped down to essentials that they possess an archetypal character, and where even now there are relatively few human artefacts to diminish one's sense of timelessness, I have come to realize that I am journeying into the deep well of my unconscious. Returning again and again to Namaqualand and the Namib has helped me to come home to the side of myself that I had never adequately explored.

Colla Swart

Cleaning up a campsite
in South Africa's
Richtersveld, 1990.

◀ Huge Atlantic breakers smash against boulders at Hondeklipbaai on the Namaqualand coast, generating and sustaining life. As the waves gradually pulverize the rock into sand and deposit it onto the beach, winds dry and lift the sand over a low rise, where it becomes part of the desert ecosystem. When the winds shift, organic debris from the desert is blown back into the sea, becoming part of the turbulent mix of nutrients that feeds aquatic life.

▶ Farther south along the coast, evening light that seems to emanate from within the rocks illuminates the ocean's spray. For me, this inner glow is an African metaphor, analogous to the inner peace of native elders who accepted the violent collision between permanent and impermanent forces in their lives as a necessary part of the creative process.

The Richtersveld is South Africa's only mountain desert, and the place where I feel most completely connected with nature. Although the Richtersveld has been traversed by vehicles and subject to grazing by goats, large areas of this extremely fragile region remain relatively undisturbed. Where there are no human artefacts to mark the years, centuries, and millennia, time seems like a circle inscribed by the seasons—having no beginning and no ending.

Many of the Richtersveld's gigantic boulders are the weathered remnants of collapsing mountains. They provide shelter and shade for a host of plants and animals and, for me, often function as powerful symbols.

◄ Colla and I have photographed this
gigantic rock many times and also
camped beneath its enormous overhang-
ing roof. Except when the wind blows,
this is a temple of silence. Each time we
depart, we endeavour to leave behind no
traces of our ever having been there.

▲ Although I had passed this spot on many
previous occasions, the circular rock had
failed to attract my attention. One April
morning I happened to walk by just as
the shadow of a huge pile of boulders
began to move across it, isolating it
visually from the background and empha-
sizing both its shape and that of the tree.

There is a striking similarity between this scattering of white rocks on a Richtersveld plain and the spacing between clumps of daisies in the Bushmanland desert (facing page). The two deserts, both part of Namaqualand, merge and fuse along their common border, often so imperceptibly that to say you are leaving one desert and entering the other is to make a claim of certainty that no geologist would attempt to defend. However, I think of the Richtersveld as a land of mountain ranges, sculpted boulders, and rocky plains, and Bushmanland as an ocean of sand punctuated here and there by buttes and mesas. The two regions evoke quite different feelings for me.

◀ Every spring (generally late July through September) the arid soil, watered by winter rains, and sometimes by snow on the mountain plateaus, comes to life. If there has been sufficient moisture, the lowveld (the dry, sandy coastal belt) blooms first, followed by the highveld (the Kamiesberge, or Kamies Mountains). Some years, sporrie (white, blue, or pale purple flax) is everywhere; other years, pink and purple mesembryanthemums are the dominant threads in the floral carpet, but every spring, orange Namaqualand daisies and ursinias sweep across the fields and up the sides of mountains. This photograph shows a mix of daisy species on a Kamiesberg farm.

▲ Seeing anything takes time, effort, and a willingness to recognize that our personal perspective is just one of many possible points of view. A termite marching across the sand might see the flowers as clouds, and a mouse might view them as we do trees. When we attempt to replicate their vision of the world, we nourish our imagination and extend our own capacity for seeing and appreciating what we see. To make this picture I lay at the edge of a field of orange gazanias, pretending to be a mouse.

My visits to Namaqualand in springtime satisfy a deep longing.
By deliberately surrounding myself with flowers, I am honouring
the part of myself that recognizes the truly beautiful to be more
valuable than the merely useful.

A mouse's-eye view of a
mesembryanthemum.

◀ In Namaqualand, even the granite blooms.

▲ Colla and I visited this rocky hillside several times over a ten-day period, and often took others with us. However, we issued our invitations carefully. Sightseers and "glancers" did not make our list. During the period of bloom, the old farmer who grazes the land, and who told us about the spot, kept his flock of sheep elsewhere.

In both this image and the one on the facing page, I deliberately kept the flowers small and emphasized the importance of their habitat in the nature story. Lichens (pioneer plants) growing on the rocks slow down the passage of air, causing sand, organic debris, and seeds to collect in the crevices. In spring, water from showers or heavy mists trickles into these natural reservoirs, causing the seeds to germinate. The rock faces shade the crevices from sun and wind, preserving the meagre water supply, so the plants can grow, bloom, set seeds, and, in the case of perennials, develop bulbs, corms, or other long-term structures. When their life cycle is completed, the plants die, but their remains enrich the soil for future generations.

Nothing in nature happens without a reason, so all natural designs describe an event or function, past or present. When I am documenting natural objects, situations, and events, I constantly examine natural visual designs—spatial relationships defined by shapes, lines, textures, and perspectives created by natural forces—for the information they contain, and endeavour to let the designs "speak" for themselves. This was my approach here.

The brick-red granite hills and outcroppings of Namaqualand are often suffused with tiny red lichens that intensify their hue. Early and late in the day, sunlight bounced into shaded areas from nearby rocks adds to the warmth of colour, which the reflected blue of the sky shifts towards purple. Chemical staining caused by moisture oozing from rock fissures and the presence of other lichens help to vary the tonal and colour scheme.

As pockets of soft rock in a granite slope were eroded by swiftly flowing water, small rocks collected in the depressions. There they were swirled around by the water, like a pestle grinding in a mortar, enlarging the holes and polishing their walls. As the water levels receded over the years, some of these beautifully sculpted rocks became collecting pools for rainwater and homes for aquatic insects and frogs. Other holes, partly filled with sand and organic materials, serve as natural containers for grasses and flowering plants.

The play of light on sand dunes
sometimes evokes comparisons with
the human body.

▲ Long after I photographed this tree and its shadow at the edge of a dune, I came to wonder if, in fact, I had unconsciously regarded them as symbols of myself and my shadow.

▶ Dunes like this advance slowly, but relentlessly. In the decade since I made this photograph, the dune has begun to bury the tree. Its fate is inevitable.

The landscape of the Great Sand Sea is stripped down to its skin. It has no clothes, no cover of grasses or trees to mask its constantly changing appearance. As Earth rotates, the sun's light is always creating new shapes, lines, and textures that, in their turn, grow, move, fade, and disappear. No other place I have visited has provided a clearer visual analogy to the physical and emotional processes of my life.

The ephemeral colour and contrasting tones of a desert sunrise often linger in my memory as music. Perhaps my sense of sight, unable to comprehend the sheer magnitude of beauty, calls on my hearing for assistance, and so I hear music in the desert silence.

THROUGH THE
LOOKING-GLASS

A CAMERA ALWAYS LOOKS BOTH WAYS. LIKE ALL SERIOUS PHOTOGRAPHERS, I HAVE to accept and deal with this fact—the reality that my images are as much a documentation and interpretation of myself as of the subject matter I choose.

Although on first viewing, an individual image, in and of itself, rarely acts as a signpost or marker of the stages of my personal development or growth, a collection of pictures provides an overview that tells the human story, and enables both myself and viewers to identify images that are representative of important changes or stages. When I am discarding old slides or negatives, I have to be careful not to throw out my life history.

There are two primary frames of reference by which I and other photographers can evaluate our work and, in the process, recognize the steps of our personal journeys. One is the subject matter or content of our images, and the other is the general treatment of that subject matter, or style. Both can be extremely instructive.

In my case there seems to have been—on a superficial viewing—relatively little change in the content of my photographs over a period of more than thirty years. But this is an illusion or a matter of labelling. Although I am still inspired most of all by natural scenes and situations and by natural things (including people), what I choose to photograph about them now is radically different in many respects from what I chose initially. Also, when viewing a few thousand of my images chronologically, I was surprised to discover that I have moved through at least four stylistic periods, three of which are significant. But these are conclusions after the fact, and they are accurate only if they are not taken too literally. The transitions are gradual, almost to the point of being imperceptible at times.

The sun glances
through a tree, near
Flinders Rangers
National Park,
Australia.

As a photographer I don't consciously select a style and then apply it to a variety of subject matter; rather, I live my life, make my images, and unconsciously document my personal journey. This suggests why my image-making rarely shows a pattern of steady improvement, but frequently is marked by periods of stasis—plateaus and ruts. I don't necessarily regard plateaus negatively, however. They may be valuable times of assimilation and consolidation after long periods or sudden spurts of personal growth. But whether I'm moving or resting, the medium always mirrors my inner self. So accurate is the reflection, that photographs often reveal the subtle beginnings of emotional transitions that I can recognize consciously only in other ways much later on.

My first photographs were realistic documentary images of familiar "things" that I liked—scenes of the St. John River, sunrises and sunsets, flowers, farm animals, and so on. I remember one day when I spent a happy hour near the door of our hen house waiting for a hen or hens to emerge and (I hoped) to peer at an egg that one of them had laid on the doorstep. When three hens suddenly emerged and stared at the egg simultaneously, I quickly pressed the shutter release and caught the moment. Later, the photograph won a number of prizes. Generally, however, my photographs were no different from pictures made by the average camera owner.

However, within a relatively short space of time I sensed that my camera (with its standard 50mm lens) was more than just a casual tool for me—even though I was basically unaware of all that I could do with it. Looking back, I realize that the early pleasure I found in recording images of things I liked was the very first indicator of what was to become a fundamental change in my career direction and, indeed, in my understanding of myself.

Speaking from hindsight, I see that the camera was a liberating tool, a socially acceptable way of saying to myself and others, especially my father, that trees and flowers and sunsets matter in and of themselves, that beauty does not need to be sacrificed on the altar of usefulness.

Although I experimented increasingly with camera positions and points of view, my formal knowledge of visual design was decidedly limited. Despite the fact that my natural sense of order helped me to make some good photographs rather early on, most of my images were visual testaments to my ignorance of design. However, things began to change rapidly for me under Helen Manzer's guidance.

Although Helen tended to be rule-oriented, her awareness of how good design made for good visual expression was clearly articulated and reinforced with practical examples. Her evaluations of photographs were specific, succinct, and always helpful. Presented with a print or transparency that left much to be desired visually, she almost never criticized, but explained how the maker could have improved on the composition. I awaited her Tuesday night classes with all the patience of a five-year-old on Christmas morning.

As I try to do in my own workshops, Helen peeled the labels off objects and spaces, and enabled me (sometimes, forced me) to see them as shapes and lines. The sky was not just sky; it was a shape within the picture space, a rectangle that could be made larger or smaller by tilting the camera up or down. A blade of grass was a line that could be oriented in a number of ways, and how it was oriented or placed in the frame influenced both the viewer's understanding of the subject matter and his or her emotional response to it. Helen made it plain that design is the craft of visual expression, that design choices must be related to image content and should always serve the purpose of communicating information or feelings about the subject matter. She did not realize the degree to which she was nourishing my soul in the process of feeding my mind. Even I, in all the excitement I was experiencing in this learning situation, couldn't have told her that.

In an effort to apply what Helen was teaching, I began to make more and more close-up pictures—of flowers, fungi, leaves, stones, and also of human constructions and manufactured objects. I needed to simplify my compositions and felt, as many others do, and all of us incorrectly, that by moving very close to something in order to photograph a small part of it, I would be working with fewer visual elements. In fact, by moving in close I made barely visible lines, shapes, and textures easier to see, so in that sense the effort was misguided, if not downright futile at times. However, the exercise had very real value for me; it made clear once and for all time that the normal human way of viewing the world is just one way of seeing.

This concentration on close-ups characterized the second (but first significant) stage in my visual growth and in my learning about the medium. Although I continued to make pictures of much larger areas and spaces, my preoccupation with close-up images continued for a number of years. And then, gradually, I began to move back, away from close-ups to the consideration of very large spaces—enormous landscapes, for example. And I found that, no matter how complicated they appeared on first viewing, I could easily see them as a few shapes (two, three, or four). The long effort to simplify, simplify, simplify had been successful. Or, to put it another way, I had learned to abstract—to recognize the fundamental visual elements of a scene without being overwhelmed by the complexities of surface details. I arrived at this third stage of visual development without actually knowing that I had arrived, so gradual was the transition. Then, in a very short space of time, I became extremely aware of what had transpired—and for a very good reason. The scene of abstraction switched from my external world to my internal one.

There is much truth in the observation that nobody sees until he or she is ready to see. However, my "seeing" was progressing on two levels and at two speeds: because of my conscious efforts, my ability to see the external physical world was developing much more rapidly than my ability to see inside myself. I have always been good at linear thinking and deductive reasoning, which helped me in this project. But life is not a line or a strand; it is, as Colla might say, a huge and enormously complex web. Yet I, like most people most of the time, recognized and dealt with only those parts of the web that presented themselves to my conscious mind. In addition to whatever personal reasons I had for not acknowledging the role the unconscious plays in my life, I was culturally conditioned to ignore or dismiss its importance.

My constant exercises in learning to simplify or, more accurately, to abstract visually probably did little *per se* to illuminate my unconscious self. However, I am convinced that these repeated conscious efforts established a pattern that my unconscious was able to "hook into" or adopt, and eventually to use as a way of bringing to consciousness aspects of myself that I had buried deeply or never examined at all. Instead of presenting itself as the vast, undifferentiated sea of dark porridge I was always imagining, my unconscious began to abstract itself into basic shapes or areas of concern that I might be able to examine consciously without too much resistance. Both archetypal and very personal dream symbols began appearing in my photographs (which I discuss in the next chapter), and, by making myself open to the messages of these symbols by reading, reflecting, and seeking the help of others, I began to gain access to new tools for redesigning life situations in more effective ways. If I had not responded positively in a conscious way to at least some of the messages contained in my photographs, I am certain that my images would have revealed my inaction.

Within the last five years or so I have developed a passionate love of texture—the weave or fabric-like nature of surfaces—which marks a fourth stage in my photographic growth. Textures are highly integrated patterns made up of tiny lines and shapes, each one of which gives up its individual identity in order to present a unified whole. I cannot help but draw a parallel between my recent love of textures and my desire to integrate the many strands and spaces of my life that I am actively examining. Not only do I consciously seek out existing textures, but I also create others that can exist only as photographic images, for example, the two-dimensional rendering of a very three-dimensional patch of grasses (lines) and the spaces (shapes) between them. Complex details now appeal to me every bit as much as basic structures did earlier—but only when the underlying whole is solid.

The appearance—indeed, the existence—of all textures is relative, depending as much on the location of the viewer as on the physical nature of whatever is being viewed. The farther away your viewing point is, the tighter the textural weave will seem to be, and if you observe the area from too great a distance you will see only a flat, undifferentiated surface. On the other hand, the closer you get to a texture, the more open or loose it will become visually—until you reach a point where both the appearance of a weave and the sense of integration are replaced by an arrangement of lines and shapes, with the surfaces of the individual shapes possibly containing new areas of texture. Again, the life parallels seem clear enough: when you get too close to a situation emotionally or remove yourself from it emotionally, you cannot experience it as an integrated whole. Both visual and emotional integration require a careful balancing of intimacy and distance.

Polarities (such as intimacy and distance, happiness and sadness, light and dark, birth and death) are common features of our lives, and therefore show up regularly in the pictures we make. For example, a shape or line in the texture field that is larger, brighter, or more colourful than all the others draws attention to itself and away from the texture. It reduces or destroys both the visual and the emotional sense of integration. Although some picture-makers regard the use of a centre of interest as a "rule of composition" (which, like all rules, terminates creative thought about the subject at hand), there are good reasons why they may want to create such an image. Perhaps some photographers will want to use texture as environment or context for the central object, illustrating a supportive role. Perhaps others will want to stress the difference or the isolation of the central object from its surroundings. In this comparison two very different, perhaps opposing goals can be achieved by adopting the same design approach.

I've long been aware that, although I am often attracted to subject matter because of the emotional effect its colours (especially secondary hues) have on me, I normally make far greater use of tones (differences in the brightness of light) when I compose an image of that subject matter. In fact, I often refer to myself as a black-and-white photographer who works in colour. Or, perhaps more accurately, I'm a colour photographer who makes constant use of tone. It's as if colours appeal to the right side of my brain, and tones to my left, or (to rephrase it slightly) the colours affect my feelings, and the tones affect my thinking. This separation is not a polarity, but rather a duality, and the challenge is to make the two aspects of the duality form a visual unity. Making a relationship work is probably a good life parallel. The most important one for me is achieving a working harmony between the two sides of myself—the unconscious and the conscious.

I draw these parallels simply to make the point that craft and art cannot be separated from life. When you point the camera's lens at your subject matter, you are also aiming it at yourself. The image you compose in the viewfinder will always be a picture of you.

Pearl Crawford

Cameras looking both ways at the Jefferson Memorial, Washington, D.C., 1962.

I made these two photographs of red lichen-covered rocks on New Zealand's South Island. The pictures are typical of the straightforward, documentary approach that I developed early but still employ frequently. My interest in and feelings for the subject matter are conveyed implicitly by the care I took in presenting it clearly—through my choice of camera position, placement of the important visual elements within the picture space, and use of maximum depth of field.

Every visual composition provides information about the composer. A careless or haphazard arrangement of material that is not random by nature reveals a superficial interest; however, if the natural arrangement is random, a caring photographer will usually endeavour to convey this visually.

As I began to understand how good visual design makes for clear visual expression, I created many close-up photographs—of rocks, leaves, flowers, and other natural and manufactured objects—believing I could more easily identify the basic shapes and lines of my subject matter. Although this exercise, which continued over a period of years, helped me to simplify my compositions, I soon realized that by enlarging a small part of an object I created new complexities. For example, when this rock face was in the sunlight, the textures in the rock showed up strongly as shapes that competed with the long, thin shape or line of the fissure.

Eventually, my persistence was rewarded. Scanning an area of any size, I found I could easily identify the basic visual components, and take a camera position that showed them to good advantage. While this rocky canyon scene is visually more complex than the facing image, I had no difficulty in perceiving the five essential areas or shapes. Once I recognized the shapes, I adjusted my camera position, allocating each a certain position and amount of picture space—all of which I had to accomplish quickly, given the movement of light and shadow.

This photograph of a palm frond is very similar in composition to the rock image on page 84, just discussed, but covers a much smaller area. The image space is divided into three shapes established by contrasting tones, with the brightest area showing a strong green hue. The picture looks relatively simple to make, but it wasn't. The frond was tossing in the wind, so I preconceived the final image and quickly pressed the shutter release at an appropriate moment.

Like the photograph on the left, this picture contains one basic hue and two major
contrasting tones. I used lines of dark tone to divide the picture space into four
related shapes. The basic simplicity of the composition enables viewers to appreciate
the more subtle tonal variations that occur in the grassy areas and give them
texture. Generally, I have found that any area, regardless of size, can be analysed as
containing one to five major shapes. Beyond that number, a composition may appear
"busy," with the shapes competing for attention. However, if I want to express
"busyness," then I may consider including more lines and shapes.

There are two ways to analyse the structure of this composition, and I considered both. One way is to regard the line or shape of brightest tone (the long shaft of ice) as the major motif or dominant visual element, and then to take a camera position that places the two parallel bands of fairly light tone (secondary lines or shapes) in visually supportive positions. The other way to view the composition is simply as alternating bands of darker and lighter tone that balance each other in a pleasing way. Whichever analysis you prefer, my intent was the same—to create a composition that expressed the natural beauty of the subject matter clearly.

Despite the vastness and complexity of the landscape, I quickly abstracted the two essential shapes—the tiny triangle formed by the pair of penguins and the huge, dark triangle of rock above it. Then, from my original position, I moved quickly to the left, so the tiny triangle was slightly to the right and the full weight of the higher and heavier triangle slightly to the left. By creating a slight imbalance (not having the two triangles positioned above and below each other vertically), I added a sense of dynamic to the composition that, in my view, is in keeping with the dynamic of the landscape.

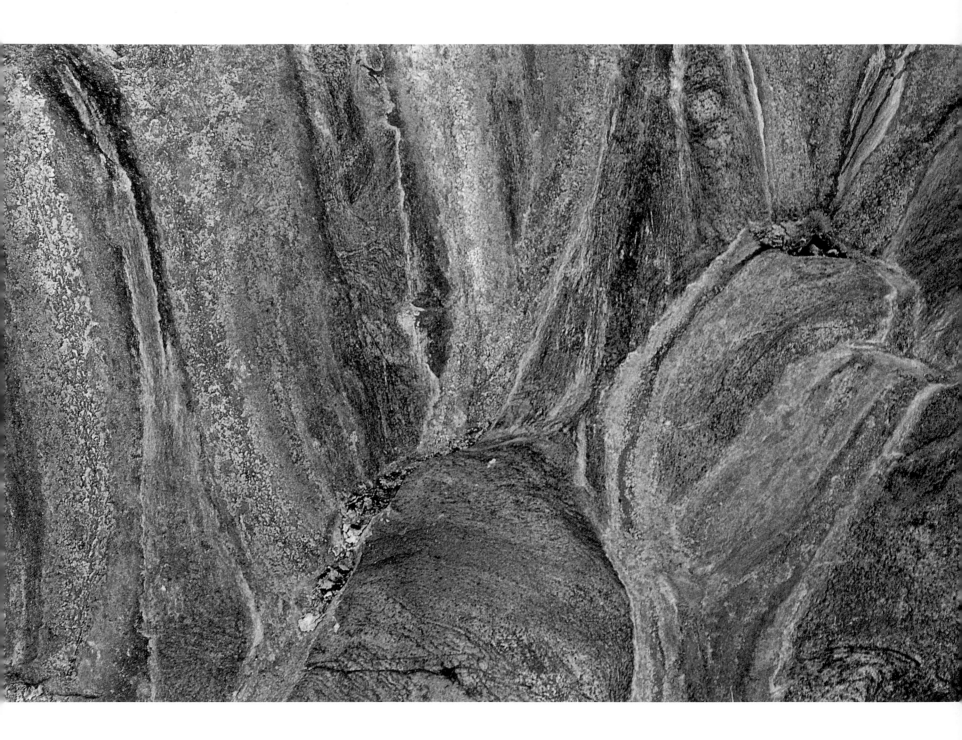

◄ This image represents something of a personal transition—an outward expression of inner movement. I have come to believe that in consciously developing my ability to identify, abstract, and arrange visual elements quickly and easily, I set up a learning pattern that my unconscious hooked into and used as a way of encouraging me to identify and examine areas of conflict and confusion that existed in my inner self. If I could do this, then I could rearrange emotional elements to create a more effective life pattern. The photograph marks a sort of halfway point—illustrating both the process of recognizing "inner lines and shapes" and the effort to integrate them.

► A light dusting of snow that partly obscures stones and bits of grass transforms my gravelled driveway into a carpet of muted hues and tones. I find this weave or fabric-like nature of a surface, which we call "texture," visually compelling, because for me it is a symbol of emotional integration. Although the image was not easy to compose, some viewers may regard it as having no design whatever. Ten years ago I would have agreed, but a decade of consciously pulling personal strands and spaces together makes me feel quite differently today.

This composition is very similar to the preceding image in its integration of visual elements, but it has one major difference. In the first photograph, which lacks colour contrast, all the tones are integrated. In this photograph, which lacks tonal contrast, the hues are integrated. But, in both, as in this stage of my life and work, I find myself consciously and unconsciously seeking out or creating examples of texture, and feel an enormous sense of satisfaction when I succeed.

This composition of the branches, leaves, and fruit of a wild hawthorn bush that grows at the foot of my driveway shows the integration of both colour and tonal contrasts. Although small shapes and thin lines remain visible, I have reduced their individual significance by using a long focal-length lens and standing at some distance from the bush. This flattening or telescoping of perspective often helps to produce or emphasize textural quality in photographs and other two-dimensional visual media.

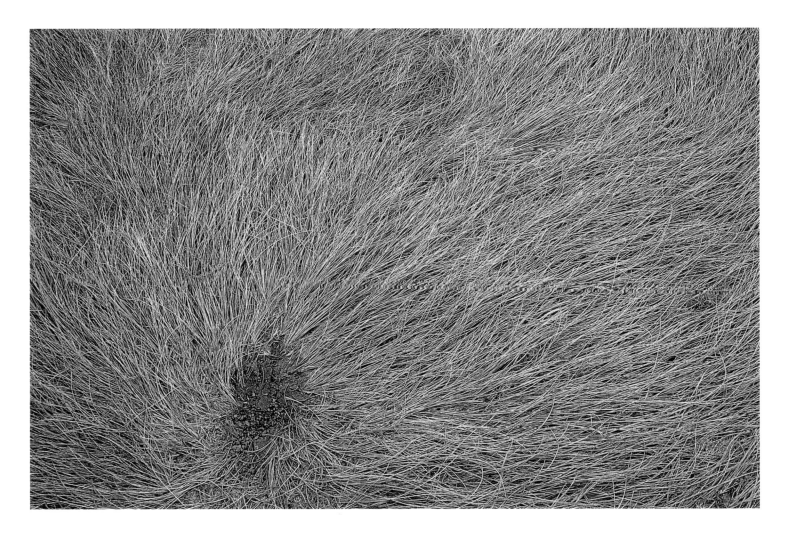

Polarities are common features of our lives and show up in the pictures we make. Take order and chaos, for example. Perfect order may be very attractive in theory, but very boring in reality. A little chaos now and then is a wonderful antidote. Perfect integration benefits from occasional interruption by a strong shape or line, because it introduces the element of change. However, to make a "rule" of such an interruption (often called a "centre of interest") is to deny the existence of polarities and the importance of personal expression.

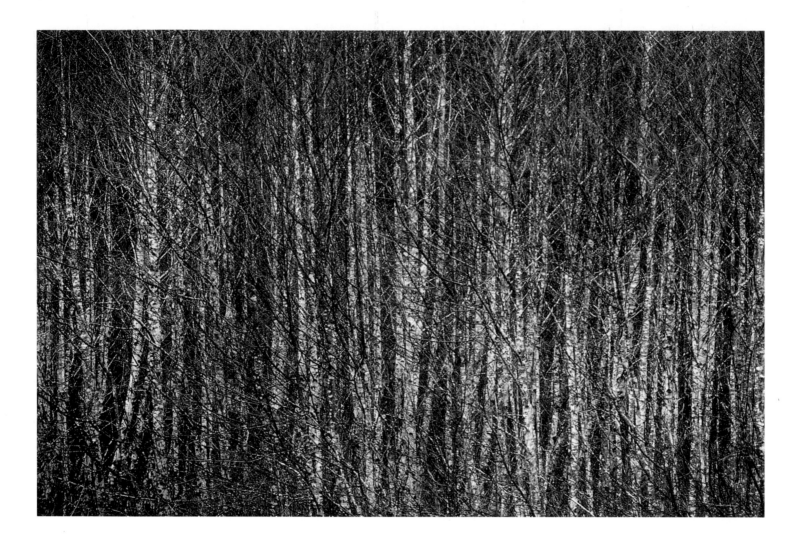

Secondary hues and subtle, restrained colour have a special emotional appeal for me.
But, even when I am working with strong, primary hues, I usually organize the
picture space around variations of tone or brightness. It's as if colours appeal to the
right side of my brain, and tones to the left. The working harmony between the
emotional and the rational that I've been able to achieve in creating photographs is
one, I hope, that I can increasingly make part of my daily life.

The very subdued colour and the textural appearance of this earthscape—the interior of an extinct volcano—were the compelling visual reasons for my photographing here. In order to prevent the texture from being overwhelmed by strong shapes, I cropped most shapes with a picture edge and used them as a "surround" for the main area of texture.

FORBIDDEN TERRITORY

I PAY A LOT OF ATTENTION TO MY DREAMS, BUT EVEN WHEN I DON'T THEIR
basic message may be conveyed to me through my photographic images in the
form of unconscious symbols. I usually file away these communications from
my unconscious with other slides, only to discover them months or years
later—when I am able to recognize them or am better equipped to understand their meaning. Other symbols occur repeatedly in my photographs over
a long period of time, but I fail to notice the repetition until, perhaps, I am
searching for a coherent series of images for an audio-visual sequence or an
instructional lecture. Only then do I recognize the symbol, which always
comes as a surprise to me, sometimes as a shock. Where have I been? What
have I been doing? Why didn't I spot this long ago? The fact is that the messages contained in a person's art often, perhaps always, precede the person's
conscious awareness of those messages.

For me, attempting to control the messages that occur unconsciously—in
dreams or pictures—by ignoring, dismissing, or deliberately trying to repress
the symbols that convey them is to engage actively in the impoverishment of
my personality. Like everybody, I am a creation of nature, and my natural
environment includes all the physical and emotional relationships in which I
have ever participated—voluntarily or otherwise. As half of this natural creation, this creature that is me, my unconscious represents my adaptation to
my natural environment.

Our early forebears accepted their unconscious as a vital aspect of themselves. They lived in close proximity to plants and animals and soil and water,

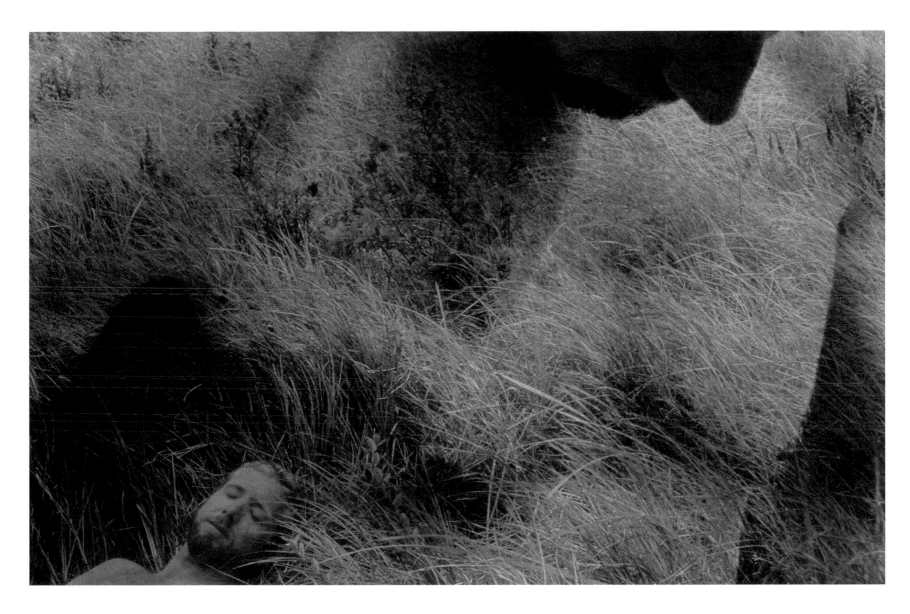

Everybody is a creation of nature, and both our conscious
and unconscious selves are vital aspects of who we are.

and in adapting to them developed strong personal and communal bonds with them, whereas we, who live apart from nature in our conscious lives, have become alienated from the wilderness within us. Nowhere, it seems to me, is this more evident than in the crowded cores of large cities, where physically and emotionally deprived people turn on each other and themselves by pillaging and burning their own environment out of sheer frustration and rage. When we are out of touch with nature—externally and internally—we are unable to integrate our conscious and unconscious selves, and necessarily condemn ourselves to being half-persons. Or, to put it positively, when we welcome wholeness by endeavouring to unite the two sides of ourselves, we are accepting or beginning to accept the fact that we are creations of nature. This is why being consciously receptive to the messages from my unconscious that appear as symbols in dreams and pictures is so important to me.

Like most people, I often find it difficult to comprehend the meaning of symbols. However, if I keep in mind that dreams—and the powerful feelings often associated with them—are meaningful only within the context of my life and that the message of every dream is related to events (often very specific events) or attitudes in my life, or to my whole life situation, then I can begin the process of understanding the message.

When I was a boy, perhaps eight or nine years old, I had a recurring dream in which I approached my father, who was facing away from me, and threw my arms around him in an embrace. In the dream he had on the old denim jacket that he often wore around our farm, but when I embraced him I discovered that nobody was inside the jacket, and the jacket itself began to fall apart.

One day, when I was about forty, I was attracted by an old, torn denim jacket of my own hanging in my porch, and although I made no connection between it and my recurring childhood dream, I experienced again a deep desire for bonding and the same feelings of loss. These feelings were so strong that I set up my tripod and camera and carefully composed the photograph you see on page 108. In hindsight, I realize that the jacket was a symbol, a message from my unconscious telling me that I still had not dealt effectively with the issue of loss or with my negative feelings for my father. Although I did not understand the symbol at the time, I had already begun to unleash some of the repressed rage I felt towards my father, a process that accelerated during the next few years.

Later, when I was planning to make a series of photographs of my biker friend Kevin, he appeared for the shooting session wearing a jean jacket as ragged as the jacket in my dream. Almost immediately I started to zero in on Kevin's jacket. But there was a difference, a big one, from the empty dream jacket: this jacket contained a body—not any body, but the healthy body of a man I respect and care about, and who was about the same age as my father when I first had my dream (see page 109). What I felt this time was not a sense of longing and loss, but one of happiness and completion. During the years between my making the two pictures, I had acknowledged and released a great deal of my anger towards my father and had come to realize that he hadn't consciously decided to wound me, that he had been wounded too, but didn't know how to acknowledge or to heal his wounds.

Although it took me a long while to recognize the symbolic content of the two jacket images and the connection between them, this experience and others like it have sensitized me to the possibility that more messages from my unconscious are appearing in my photographs, thus helping me to spot them more quickly. However, although we reveal something of ourselves in every picture we make—indeed, in all our creative endeavours—I am very careful to avoid labelling every bush, bird, house, or jacket that I photograph as being an important symbol from my unconscious.

I've found that sometimes I can recognize the significance of a visual symbol only when the symbol (and often a particular use or placement of it) occurs repeatedly in my photographs, as in a recurring dream. Recently, while sorting through images from several countries made during the 1980s and early 1990s, I was amazed to discover, scattered through my files, a significant number of compositions in which I had included a large circular rock as the powerful focal point of an earthscape or a natural scene. Some of these circular rocks (or globes) are so similar in appearance that a viewer could be forgiven for asking if I keep an earth mover in my camera bag, or if I had transported the rock from a glacier high in the Andes to a beach in the Bahamas by computer manipulation. (I hadn't.)

The circle is the most perfect of all shapes, and an archetypal symbol. It appears in the visual art of every culture and may variously represent, for example, the self (one's spiritual centre or the innermost nucleus of the psyche, sometimes referred to as "the soul"), an egg or embryo (the promise of birth), a sense of wholeness or completion (which, like an embryo, is related to the development of the self). The important thing for me to consider was the symbol's possible meaning for me during this period. What was occurring in my life, in my self's development, that could best be represented by a circle? Was this something I desired or needed? Was it an attempt at self-healing on the part of my unconscious? Or was it something that, at least to some extent, I had achieved? The possible answers are important: only when the ego (the conscious being) notices, contemplates, and acts upon messages from the unconscious self can one hope to grow.

I have come to see the self as a seed that contains the whole plant in latent form, but the plant can develop only when the seed is exposed to light and provided with the air, water, and soil of daily life. Because life conditions or circumstances differ (ample light and water, but poor-quality soil, for example), the plant that grows from the seed has the potential of a million variations. By analogy, the more conscious attention I can give to providing good growing conditions for the plant that is me, the healthier and more whole a person I will become.

One of the things that most intrigues me about the appearance of the single round rock in my photographs is that, like an abstract circle, it represents the self. It is a trans-cultural symbol that can also be very personal. What I am dealing with here is both "the" self and "my" self.

Furthermore, the very strong or dominant placement of the round rock in a variety of large scenes or environments is significant. I feel that it can be directly related to a conscious decision I made about fifteen years ago to identify situations and experiences that I feared, and then to put myself in those situations or have those experiences in order to overcome my fear of them or, more accurately, the fear behind them. My reason for doing this was simple enough—I had come to realize that I could never hope to occupy emotional territory (to feed my self, to grow, to become more whole) in which I was afraid to venture. However, I would be less than honest if I were not to acknowledge that this conscious decision to act was itself preceded by a period of growth in which I had gradually faced up to various anxieties.

In examining my photographs of the last five years, I notice that the appearance of a single round rock placed in a large environment has become much less frequent. The dominant emphasis now—and my passion—is for texture, which I discussed in the preceding chapter. This visual integration of shapes and lines into a weave or fabric seems to suggest a period of personal integration. Although initially my unconscious provided the visual messages, this time "the conscious I" recognized them more quickly than it had ever done before.

I still collect rocks and stones in my photographs—however, mostly in Africa. There is a beach on the coast of Namaqualand sloped at precisely the right angle for incoming waves to roll rocks and small boulders up to higher ground, only to have them roll back again as the water recedes. The continual ominous thunder of tumbling rocks is enough in itself to stir deep emotions, but the rounded, polished rocks that lie exposed when the tide is out evoke a sense of the unalterable, the immortal, of a complete and lasting self.

I also collect rocks in the Richtersveld, South Africa's mountain desert. These natural skyscrapers, some perhaps thirty storeys high, are the eroded and weathered remnants of mountain ranges heaped together in massive piles, the burial mounds of ancient Nama gods. On my very first visit to one of these places, I spent the day alone—hiking, climbing, and photographing. Returning to the camp-fire that night, I said to my friend Colla, "I know this place. I feel that I've been here before. I can tell what's on the other side of a boulder before I walk around it."

Once I spent an entire day in the Richtersveld bringing huge round boulders together, making them touch, almost embrace each other, by careful selection of camera positions. Although initially I was not conscious of what I was doing, I gradually became more and more aware as the soft sidelighting of early morning intensified to the blazing light of noon. In a world of powerful natural symbols, messages from the self can penetrate consciousness with a rapidity uncommon in cultures hooked on technology. In the years since my first visit, I've returned to this spot several times. No other place on Earth gives me such a feeling of belonging, and nowhere have I photographed with a greater sense of inner excitement and pervading joy than in this land of rocks. At night I lie in my sleeping-bag beneath a curving canopy of granite, following my rotation around the sun by observing the movement of the billion stars that shimmer in the undiluted blackness of an unpolluted sky, and feel peace.

Across the Orange River from the Richtersveld, in Namibia, vast expanses of red sand stretch, undulate, and rise among the mountains. The earthscape is so exquisitely beautiful that, from my emotional and aesthetic perspective, no human being should ever have been allowed to defile it. But alluvial diamonds are found here, and large portions of the coastal regions have been reserved for and managed by mining companies for the last century. It is called "The Forbidden," or "The Prohibited," Territory—Die Sperrgebiet—but whether that is because visitors are not allowed or because the climate is so hostile I do not know. There are ghost towns in Die Sperrgebiet, only one of which is readily accessible to the public, but after many years I have been able to visit them all, thanks to the kindness of a geologist–manager who is a fine amateur photographer.

Built by German mining companies in the early years of this century, for two or three decades these towns were pockets of European culture stitched onto the shifting sands of the Namib desert. There were houses, schools, offices, and, of course, mine buildings. In Kolmanskop there was a hospital and, both here and in Elisabethbaai, huge and elegant recreation halls, containing facilities for stage productions, sports, and dining. Now the doors stand open, most of the window glass has been shattered, roofs are missing or partly missing, the brightly painted walls have been sand-blasted—and the sand drifts through and through. Although I am pleased that almost no attempt has been made to preserve the abandoned buildings, since to me their very presence represents human beings out of touch with nature, their now-ghostly appearance and the sound of the wind sucking through cracks and rattling loose boards symbolizes the fate that we can all expect unless we reconnect with Earth. Because every symbol (in order to function as a symbol for someone) is laden with emotional energy, no amount of time is enough time for me to photograph the ghost towns.

But not everybody feels about them as I do. When I visited Elisabethbaai with five photographers, two members of our group found the scene so depressing that they made almost no pictures, and another, experiencing no particular emotion, wandered about rather aimlessly. For me, the ocean mists that swirled around and partly obscured the colourful shells of row houses evoked the feelings of a bomb site. I wondered about the different life experiences that each of us brought with us to the town that day, conditioning our responses, and concluded that we were all affected by the scene, even the photographer who seemed unable to react. Once again I was forcefully reminded that a symbol can be felt and understood only within the context of our individual lives.

Ian Samson

The image of this scene long had a mysterious attraction for me. Years passed before
I came to recognize its symbolic character. Viewing the picture as a unit, a whole, I
now regard the white cloud rising out of the darkness as a part of my unconscious
self being exposed to the light of consciousness.

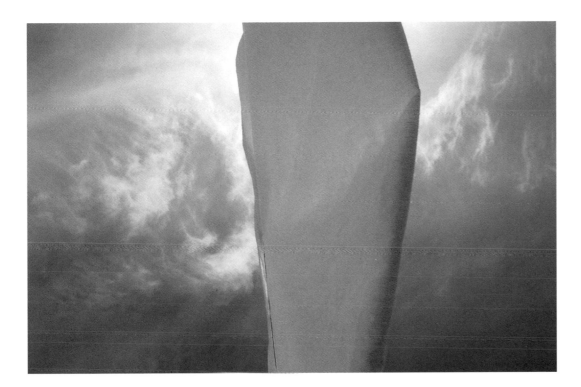

I made this photograph several years after the one on the facing page, but it languished in my files until, one day, its relationship to the preceding image struck me with sudden emotional force. The white cloud, still mysterious, had taken on a more definite shape. I realized that this was not accidental, and I asked the question that many viewers ask: "What is it?" (A sheet hanging on a line, viewed from the ground—but, of course, that's not the point.)

These denim jackets are dream symbols that showed up in my photographs as initially unconscious responses to opposing aspects of the same situation. I did not understand my emotional reactions until much later, when I remembered that such a jacket was a powerful symbol for my relationship with my father that had first surfaced in a recurring childhood dream. The first jacket is empty, dead; the second, literally full of life (see page 100).

◄ Over a period of about ten years I made
many photographs of round rocks, boulders, and other circular objects without
ever being aware of how frequently I was
doing it. When I started sorting through
thousands of pictures for a particular
project, I soon spotted what I had been
doing, and began asking myself what the
circle represented that was so important
to me during this period of my life.

▶ Did I photograph these ostrich eggs lying
abandoned in the desert because the
scene was so unexpected, so surreal? Or,
were both the circles and the desert—the
entire situation—of symbolic importance
for me? Why do I choose the subject
matter I do? Why do I photograph it in
the manner I do? These are the sorts of
questions that photographs ask of the
photographer who makes them.

I have concluded that my repeated use of the circle was a healthy process of self-understanding originating in my unconscious. Symbols that occur repeatedly in pictures or dreams become less frequent or disappear altogether when the factors that cause their occurrence are identified and dealt with emotionally.

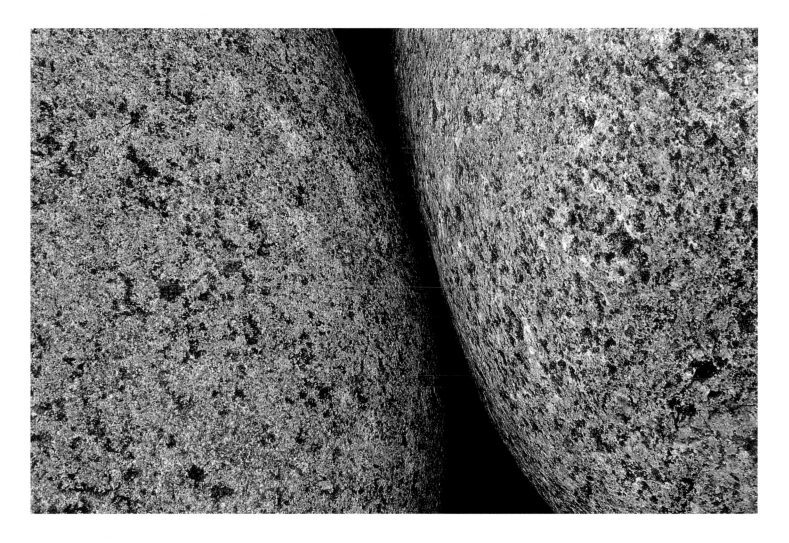

I doubt that I have ever made a simpler composition than this—two rocks of approximately equal importance touching, bridging the darkness between them. Considering the pleasure I felt photographing in this situation and the utterly uncomplicated nature of the image, I can only conclude that my picture of the rocks is not a longing for intimacy, but an expression of connectedness—of feeling at one with myself and the world I inhabit.

A major difference between this photograph and the one on the preceding page is that only one rock curves towards the other. The second rock remains straight, stiff, unyielding. Another major difference is that the space between the rocks is lighter, not darker, than they are. A third difference is the presence of the shrub (an olive species, by the way) that, like the curving rock, reaches towards the rigid stone. These visual differences suggest a message different from that of the previous image.

There are a number of ways I could have made this image—by double exposure, by sandwiching two identical slides or negatives together while reversing one in the process, or by computer manipulation. But, how I made the picture is far less important than the fact that I made it. The tools and techniques of any medium that are the means for expressing a feeling or idea are ultimately secondary to the feeling or idea itself.

Die Sperrgebiet

Since we all have many experiences in common, we share many symbols—light as a symbol of hope, and darkness as a symbol of despair, for instance. However, because symbols can be felt and understood only within the context of our individual lives, and because every symbol (in order to function as a symbol for someone) is laden with emotional energy, objects or experiences that are symbolic for me may well have greater or lesser symbolic value for others. This explains why the few people who have visited the ghost towns of Namibia's Die Sperrgebiet (The Forbidden Territory) often respond with quite dissimilar feelings.

For me, these long-abandoned towns pictured on the following pages trigger such powerful emotions that I prefer to wander about photographing them alone.

I find it painful to watch people who do not share my feelings racing from one building to another, making snapshots while obliterating the tracery of wind on sand with sets of footprints that, for a while at least, destroy the sense of the past. When I am alone or with somebody who feels much as I do, the ghosts of the past return. Sometimes, the non-existent sound of familiar German drinking songs resonates so strongly through the empty halls that I conjure up the miners who celebrated over beer at the end of yet another gruelling week, or imagine the laughter of the children who built castles in the sand.

CREATION AND CREATIVITY

SOMETIMES WHEN I'M RELAXING IN AN EASY CHAIR OR SITTING ON MY FRONT deck gazing down across fields to the river and the hills, I find myself asking what really matters to me, and trying to put these things in perspective. These moments of reflection are usually good times for me, because I don't consciously cause them to happen or force them to last any longer than seems natural. They are also essential times. It's important to gather up the many strands of one's life now and then, and prepare to do a bit of weaving. Or, perhaps, to examine how personal tapestries already woven are integrated into and influenced by larger social and cultural patterns—to ask where one fits in, and where one wants to fit. So, now and then, I find it very useful to extend the initial moments of reflection by deliberately focusing for a few hours or days on the content of those moments, rather than letting this conscious material slip back, unexamined, into my unconscious.

Trying to find the answers and perspective I'm seeking often means engaging in some research, and before long my kitchen table gets heaped with books on religion, philosophy, ecology, genetics, dreams, the nature of creativity, art history, biography, and whatever else seems relevant. I don't read many of them from cover to cover, but sniff and plunge like a fox after a mouse. I highlight paragraphs with a felt pen, mark pages, make notes, and then transfer some of the chaos to my computer, where it sits—marinates, I sometimes think—until I'm in an organizational mood. Although I realize that my understanding of my life and its context will always be extremely limited, from my initial musings to the time when I am able to gain some new

The universe in progress:
a four-hour exposure of
the night sky.

insights into "the big picture," I feel a quiet, pervading sense of excitement, because fundamentally this weaving project or process is a conscious search for meaning.

I'm a photographer, but as a good friend of mine is fond of saying when he's labelled as being this or that, "I'm a person first." So the question often arises as to why I find my photography so important—and fulfilling—to me, the person. In preceding chapters I have endeavoured to identify and examine consciously some of the unconscious connections, but here I want to deal with the conscious connections, to view them rationally, and to state certain conclusions that are important to me.

My first concern as a photographer is to know my craft. This has two essential aspects: use of visual design, and use of the camera and related tools. Craft is a conscious, often intellectual, but usually very practical endeavour. A person learns the tools and techniques for sculpting, or acting, or composing and making photographs, then uses these tools and practises these techniques repeatedly until they become second nature, just like learning to drive a car. And anybody who cares seriously about his or her craft will always be endeavouring to learn new techniques or to improve old ones. A pianist who, one evening in a concert hall, profoundly moves the audience with her seemingly effortless rendition of a particular sonata will very likely be back at the piano the following day repeatedly practising certain passages in order to maintain and improve the quality of her craft.

Like the pianist, being a good craftperson matters to me. It matters for the craft itself, but it also matters because craft, especially good craft, makes art possible. For me, art is the message (feelings, passions, caring arising from the unconscious) that is given form, defined, or expressed through craft. Or, to put it another way, craft is the vehicle for art. For example, the horror of a nightmare can be described in words (craft of writing), in a ballet (craft of dance), or in a picture (craft of photography, painting, or drawing). Generally speaking, when a person is so thoroughly familiar with and experienced in a craft that working in it is an almost automatic process, his or her feelings are relatively unimpeded by the formal demands of the medium, which means that the artistic message—the passionate caring of the creator or performer of a work—is expressed clearly. (Whether or not the message is received, however, depends not only on the creator or performer, but also on the viewer, listener, or reader of the work.)

Because the term "artist" implies a quality of soul, or an appeal to the human spirit, or an insight or feeling that is expressed through the craftwork a person produces, I'm always pleased when painters, sculptors, actors, dancers, musicians, and photographers describe themselves in terms of their craft or profession, rather than call themselves artists, which seems to me a potentially dangerous indulgence of one's ego or a plea for recognition. Writers and athletes don't refer to themselves as artists (though others may), nor do a host of other craftpersons who, to my mind, are every bit as entitled. Because learning a craft well demands enormous mental energy, painstaking attention to detail, and endless physical practice, I believe we can take genuine personal pride in calling ourselves precisely what we are— and let other people decide whether or not they want to call us artists. If they do, we can draw strength from the fact that, through our pictures, we are communicating our caring for our subject matter and sharing the feelings it generates in us.

Even the most widely recognized artists are craftpersons most of the time—indeed, they have to be. If the pianist I mentioned doesn't practise regularly, there is little possibility that she will be able to continue using her chosen medium to express her feelings in a passionate or caring way. In workshops on photography and visual design, I constantly encourage participants to practise, practise, practise—to give themselves assignments on a regular basis—so they can avoid the frustration of having to relearn the use of tools and techniques, and express themselves clearly, when they find themselves in situations that really matter to them.

Of course, some activities have more potential for artistic expression than others, though I tend to interpret this fact liberally, never rigidly. The main intent of mechanics and farmers, for instance, is to produce something of practical usefulness, whereas an artist creates something that, ostensibly, is of spiritual value. It is this appeal to the spiritual centre, or soul, that connects art to religion, and explains why the edifices of many great religions are expressions or repositories of great art.

I have never found a better general definition of religion than Paul Tillich's "ultimate concern about ultimate things." It not only describes the essence of religion, but also explains the basic difference between religion and art. In effect, Tillich would say that, while all art deserving of the name is characterized by profound caring, only some art expresses ultimate concern about ultimate things.

Because I care deeply about the quality and meaning of my life, and about both the physical and the non-physical environment that makes my life possible, I think of myself as a religious person. Although I have no affiliation with any organized religious group, and am rarely to be found in a place of formal worship, I am an active "seeker."

For me, the antithesis of religion is passivity or non-involvement. In my view, a person who believes in God and attends church regularly, but who habitually spends afternoons or evenings (often both) parked in front of a television set watching soap operas and sit-coms, is essentially non-religious. Where is the ultimate concern about ultimate things in such a life pattern? Where is the creativity that is revealed in Creation—from the incomprehensibly vast and dynamic universe, to the passionate application of paint to canvas, to the first, hesitant steps taken by a very young child? Regardless of whether we are theists, atheists, or agnostics, the scripture of Creation—the most sacred of all texts—lies open before us every moment of our lives, waiting to be read. It tells the story of the creative process.

My friend, educator Susan Kiil, described the creative process succinctly and beautifully when she wrote: "The creative process is at work in everything that happens in the Universe. It is in the cycles of nature, in our relationship with the planet and with each other, and in all our thoughts and feelings. The creative process is constantly linking the elements of Earth and emotions and ideas into new patterns and cycles. And when these new forms have fulfilled their need, they die and provide the beginning of new forms. This is the process of eternal renewal, the energy that links everything in the

Epiphany at Shamper's Bluff.

universal web of life." Our ability to be creative human beings is inextricably tied into Creation itself.

The eco-theologian Father Tom Berry speaks to us about the linkage between Creation and creativity when he says, "The more we diminish the planet, the more we diminish ourselves." He is talking about how our spiritual condition depends on our physical resources, because he goes on to ask where, if we lived on the moon, we would find the materials to build a violin. Since the materials do not exist there, we would be deprived of the whole range of string music, from Bach concerti to the "down home" fiddle tunes to which so many of us have danced—and we would be spiritually poorer as a result.

The most important connection between craft, art, and religion is that they are all concerned with creativity and creation. The most important differences between craft and art have to do with their origins (broadly speaking, consciousness versus unconsciousness) and their goals. However, although religious concern—ultimate caring about ultimate things—is more easily expressed in art than in craft, especially craft that is pursued mainly for practical purposes, it is not captive to it. Potentially, we can find religious concern anywhere. This is because, in our heart of hearts, we all ask the question about the purpose and meaning of existence (especially our own)—and we attempt to answer it even by consciously ignoring the question or denying its importance. This is an issue from which we may consciously hide, but from which we can never escape, because it always remains firmly rooted in our unconscious self, emotionally linked to our instinct for self-preservation. We would rather be than not be.

Photography—both the craft and the art—helps me to be. It allows and enables me to live creatively, which is to honour Creation and my own existence. As I consciously pursue my craft, my concerns, anxieties, fears, loves, hopes, and dreams bubble up from my unconscious. In this meeting of the conscious and the unconscious, I can acknowledge my wounds and experience healing. Photography is neither a religion nor a panacea, but it provides me with the opportunity of "growing towards wholeness." And that, surely, is what the religious quest is all about.

There may well have been universes before this one and universes that will follow it, each creation beginning with an explosion of energy so enormous that it expands for billions of years by human time. Then, when the energy is so dispersed that it can no longer support the structure, the universe collapses and contracts to re-form the dense concentration of energy that will cause another "Big Bang." Although we can only speculate, it is not unreasonable to think that a new universe is born at the moment an old one dies.

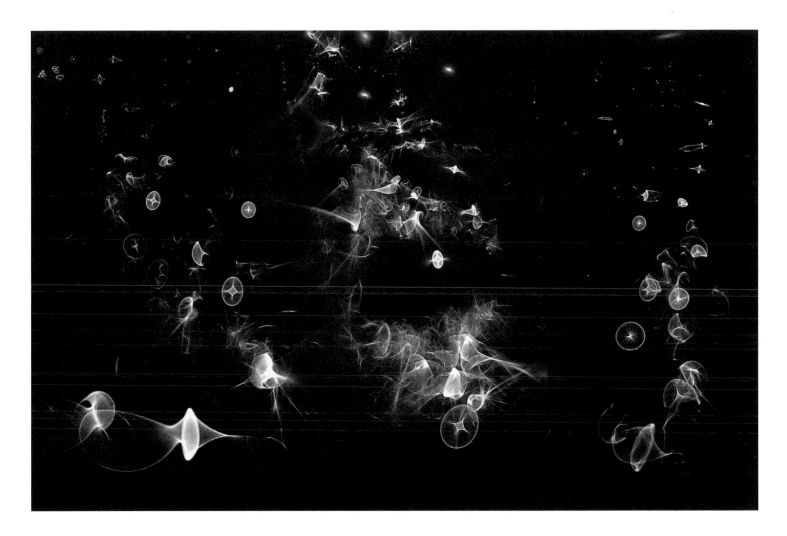

Difference is the fundamental law of the universe. Without differences the universe would be a perfectly static place—no change, no growth. But, because of differences, everything is possible. For example, light has form and meaning only because of darkness, and darkness because of light. Together they provide the dynamic of a creative process, and creation can occur, as in this photograph.

◄ Both of the two preceding images and this one were made right around my home. The flares and spots of light shining in the dark (preceding page) are simply out-of-focus, back-lighted water-drops on leaves in my garden. The other two photographs show the effects of light shining through glasses of coloured water onto kitchen foil. Although this informa-tion may put the brakes on your imagina-tion or perhaps reduce your capacity for responding emotionally to the images, I hope they demonstrate that I've found no better place for making photographs than wherever I am.

► The exercises in seeing and use of design that I practise at home, where I usually can take the time to consider my compo-sitions thoughtfully, free me up for the many other occasions when I have to translate my response to subject matter into quickly executed designs. Flying over Australia's Whitsunday Island was one of those occasions. Both the small plane I was in and the light patterns were mov-ing rapidly.

◀ The creative process always involves
death—death in our environment, the
deaths of family members and friends,
and, one hopes, the death of personal life
patterns that inhibit emotional and
intellectual growth.

▲ Grieving and remembering are ways of
adjusting to death, of dealing with it
emotionally, and ultimately of making
it a positive, creative force in our lives.

I could not pass this situation by. Not wanting to alter it more than was necessary to record it clearly, I first selected a camera position that allowed the secondary circles to support the circle of the frying pan. Then I moved the handle just enough to create an oblique line pointing in from the upper left, rather than keeping it as a vertical line coming from the top.

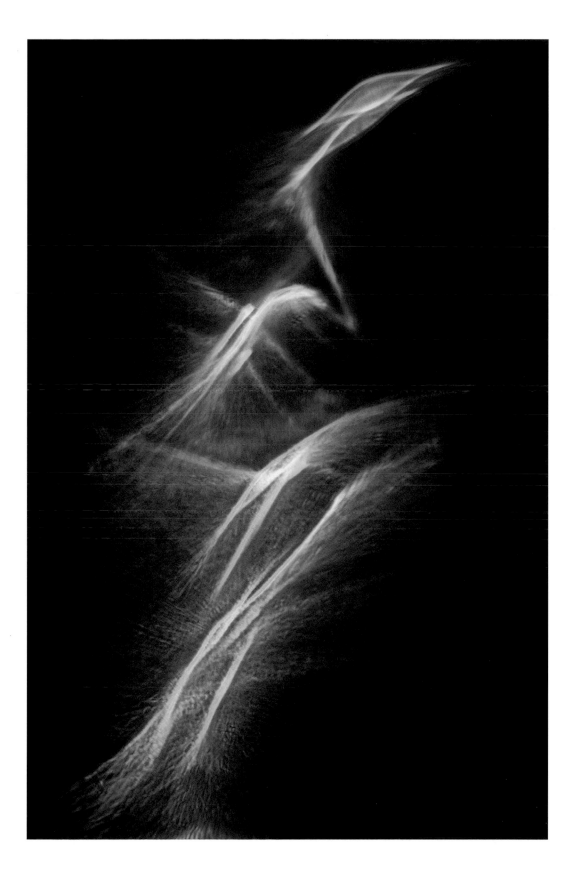

Life and death are polarities that raise the question of the meaning of existence—in both the general and the personal sense. They have supreme emotional force. Recently, as a result of having to face the possibility of imminent death, I took control of my life in new, important ways. The dead bird in the frying pan helped me to create this "great bird of light," one of my most recent photographs, made by exploring a plain glass paperweight.

INNER HIGHWAYS

ONE VERY CHILLY MORNING WHEN I WAS MOTORCYCLING THROUGH NEW ZEALAND a few years ago, I pulled into a lay-by to warm up. The only other people around were a middle-aged couple having breakfast at a picnic table. As soon as they realized I was going to park my bike, they quickly gathered up their food and stood beside their car. And when I unbuckled my metal tripod from the top of a saddle-bag in order to make some pictures of the scenery, they departed in a cloud of dust—probably expecting to be struck by a bullet at any moment.

A lot of people used to think that biking was out of character for me—especially when they saw me riding by on my Harley-Davidson or at a function of some sort clad head to toe in black leather and carrying a helmet under my arm. Not so many people think that way any more, which pleases me for a couple of reasons. For one thing, I dislike being stereotyped as much as does anybody else, yet nearly everybody lives in ways that make labelling easy. "He's a photographer" or "She's a bank manager" or "They're bikers" identifies activities that all too often are thought to presuppose a certain lifestyle and kind of character, when in fact they tell us next to nothing about a person. When I started getting into serious biking, friends, acquaintances, and relatives began to take another look at me, which brings up the second reason for my being glad that they no longer regard my motorcycling as being out of character. Because the "me" they knew hadn't changed for the worse, just "expanded," so to speak, they had to dump their preconceptions about who's a biker.

Ever since I bought my Harley (I owned another large motorcycle before that), I've been struck by the number of people who, quite deliberately, pull

Biker doing a "burn-out," New Brunswick, Canada.

their car or truck in beside my bike in a half-empty parking lot or at a gas pump, lean out the window, and almost invariably remark, "Nice bike you got there." I've never kept a tally of their ages, or the kinds of cars they drive, or anything else about them, for that matter, but one day it occurred to me that, if I had to describe the typical guy (although it's not always a man), I'd probably say, "He's forty years old, married, has 2.2 kids, and attends religious services at least occasionally." And he has a yearning, because something he wants in life, something he may never have identified consciously, is passing him by—and he's letting it happen.

Quite frankly, there's something in everybody that wants to be a "biker." It's a longing for the freedom that motorcycles, especially Harleys, have come to represent, a desire that is all too often sublimated, lying buried in the unconscious for decades, or perhaps one's entire life. The bike and the biker titillate the secure and the comfortable and disturb the repressed, because freedom of any sort, like motorcyling, involves taking risks. It is often more convenient emotionally to resent the symbol than to examine the source of the discontent or the cause of the resentment. Or, easier to acknowledge the power of the symbol if you can accompany it with an excuse for not embracing it: "I'd love to have a bike like yours, but my wife won't hear of it." Whatever the guy is talking about, it certainly isn't about bikes. Such confessions of longing for a Harley, which can be interpreted as the desire to take personal control of one's life, come easily to many people when the reason for the yearning can be masked or directed away from one's self.

The flip side of the coin is a biker rally. There, perfectly ordinary people let their (often very long) hair down as far as it will go. They assault taboos by specializing in outrageous and ridiculous behaviour—wearing cattle horns on their helmets, skunk pelts for caps, or very high leather boots with a bikini for accompaniment. They flaunt their tattoos. They challenge each other in nonsensical bike games like "the wienie bite" and "the balloon toss," getting slathered with mustard or drenched with water in the process. They drink too much beer, dance on tables, and trade T-shirts. Maybe none of them has control of his or her life, maybe some of them do, but for a little while at least they live their symbol of freedom, and for most of them the experience is healthy and good. I have often tried to capture the spirit of a biker rally in photographs, but I have always failed. Most rallies are simply too big and chaotic. All I can capture are snippets of liberation and belonging—anything more than that eludes me. Besides, I'm usually having too much fun dancing or just hanging out.

One of the things I like most about bikers is that, for the most part, they treat everybody the same. Nobody's special, and everybody is quick to help each other out. It doesn't matter if you're a computer programmer, a mechanic, a stockbroker, a nurse, or a photographer—your vocation is irrelevant. So are your net worth, your marital status, and your physical appearance. For the time you're together, bikes and biking and having fun are all that matter. The community has a core, and everybody knows and wants it to be what it is.

I've had the most success in making pictures when I'm photographing one or two bikers at a time. Bikers in a group are bikers; they tend to show, or even flaunt, the biker stereotypes. On the other hand, a biker by himself is a living, breathing human being, a person. When you ride together or tinker with your machines, you get the same grease on your jeans. Before long you're probably sharing a beer. At times like these the objective act of making photographs is the last thing I have in mind, but sometimes I become so aware of how a person's mood or feelings (his subjectivity) are imaged in his facial expressions, gestures, and other body movements that, depending on my own feelings, I may ask to make some pictures.

Biking has everything to do with feelings. I didn't get on a motorcycle because I wanted to think, however necessary thinking is to riding well. I got on one because my emotions put me there. Biking and its associated activities are a form of play for me, something I had far too little opportunity to engage in as a child and a lack which, as an adult, I've decided to rectify. But these emotions were quickly augmented by feelings of another sort—those aroused by the sensory experiences of riding. My body became engaged, and the whole thing got very physical.

I can see more and I can see it better from a motorcycle than from a car travelling at the same speed. Because I have to be more alert for dangers to my personal safety, my eyes are constantly scanning not only the road ahead, but everything on both sides—a tiny patch of loose gravel, a dog running across a lawn, all the driveways I'm going to pass in the next nine seconds and, as I relax into the ride, the blue pond in the middle of a green marsh, a carpet of wildflowers or grasses twisting through a grove of trees, and every damn power line that cuts across my field of vision.

In spring I ride through erogenous zones of aromas and fragrances—the lilt of apple blossoms and lilacs in the air, the pure breath of rapidly flowing streams, the raw earthiness of freshly ploughed soil. In summer I slow down for the sweet scent of newly mown hay, or race home because I can sniff the coming rain and, if the first drops fall before I reach my destination, I roll my tongue around my lips to savour the wetness. In autumn the pungent tang of highbush cranberries and rotting leaves provokes deep feelings of fulfilment and of sadness. It's been a great ride, but I'm approaching the end of the road.

On a motorcycle I feel the warmth of the sun shining on my back suddenly interrupted by the coolness of a cloud's shadow. I freeze when a night wind picks up and I'm still dressed for the afternoon. I swelter in my leathers as the morning temperature climbs through warm to hot—because I'm loath to stop for the few minutes it will take to remove them.

And I hear with my whole body. The roar of the accelerating engine reverberates off the walls of a highway underpass or a tunnel of buildings in a sudden, erotic, staccato blast. Many bikers, especially men, experience the sound of their machines as the most sensual—and often, sexual—sensation of riding. It arouses the animal within the leather, the wild creature, and brings them closer to nature and their natural, unacculturated selves than a quiet lake or an awesome sunset ever can. All of this can be very difficult to admit, of course, which is why so many bikers divert attention from their feelings by wearing helmet decals that read: "Loud Pipes Save Lives." Personally, despite my dislike of noise pollution, I have to acknowledge that the sound of my Harley intensifies the emotional experience of riding. I can no more imagine riding a silent motorcycle than I can contemplate putting a motor on a canoe.

I'm definitely not into biking because, somehow, it will make me a more perceptive and sensitive photographer. I'm into it because, risks aside or risks included, I enjoy it. Motorcycling and the companionship of bikers put me in touch with important feelings; they stretch my sensory capacity, and develop my appreciation for the sensual. But these things also affect both what I see and how I see it. My eyes work best when I engage—and enjoy—my other senses as well, especially when I regard them as companions, not as servants of my eyes. And I am more holistically aware when I treat my senses, with their enormous capacity for connecting me with my emotions, as partners of my intellect. The Jesuit admonition to put reason above passion no longer cuts any ice with me.

A couple of years ago it occurred to me that it would be great fun to bring together the members of my bike group and the members of a local camera club. Bikers always like to have good pictures of themselves with their machines, and serious amateur photographers are usually keen to take advantage of unusual opportunities. We decided to have the photo shoot at my home on a Sunday in early June. The arrangement was that each biker would model with his or her bike, and in return would receive a large colour print of himself or herself, and (at the biker's own expense) any number of prints or "snaps." Also, the camera-club members volunteered to produce an audio-visual record of the event to show at both the camera club and the bike club.

I asked the photographers to come early (about twenty turned up), so I could give them a few visual and photographic tips by showing and discussing some of my slides of bikers and bike events. Then we gathered on my front deck for an overview of my very long, sloping driveway, so everybody could set up tripods and otherwise get ready for the sudden influx. (I knew that the first forty bikers would be arriving as a group, riding in the standard staggered formation that makes for safer riding on a highway.) The photographers were barely in place before they could hear the roar of Harleys in the distance.

Eventually there were sixty-seven motorcycles, and an uncounted number of bikers and passengers (mostly partners and children) scattered through the fields around my house. My dog made visits to them all, then located the geographic centre of activity, stretched out in the grass, and pretended to be asleep. There was much shouting, the frequent revving of engines, and music coming from somewhere—all the chaos of a community picnic or a family reunion. Some bikers lunched with photographers on the deck, other bikers posed patiently until the photographers were satisfied, but many extended their modelling sessions by offering photographers a creative range of extra poses or some cold beer, while a few curled up in the shade and slept off the last vestiges of Saturday night. Generally, the bikers took it easy, but the photographers (outnumbered almost four to one) were kept busy all afternoon. Nevertheless, many of them got to know and enjoy each other, especially a financial counsultant/photographer who discovered he was making pictures of a financial consultant/biker. As the last of the bikers roared away just before dark, one of them paused long enough to shout at me over the din, "You know, these photographers are good people!"

On my Harley, 1993.

Andrew Clyde Little

◄ Harley-Davidson motorcycles, Daytona Bike Week, Florida, U.S.A.

► A young "headbasher" and "biker wannabe" displays his rings, Wellington, New South Wales, Australia.

"Ruffy," near Melbourne, Australia.

Biker family at Australia's National H.O.G. (Harley Owners' Group) rally.

Pause for refreshment at the famous Ettamogah Pub, Australia. (Like every biker-tourist, I parked my bike nearest the camera.)

Rian taking a smoke break, Kamiesberg Pass, South Africa.

Kevin with his Harley, New Brunswick, Canada.

Kevin in a reflective moment, New Brunswick, Canada.

HOME

A FEW NIGHTS AGO MY OLD AND FAITHFUL COMPANION TOSCA, A GERMAN shepherd, was walking up a path in front of the house after warning a small herd of deer that they were grazing too close for comfort. As she neared the deck, she had a heart attack, lay down, and died. The next morning I loaded her body onto a wheelbarrow and, with my sister and aunt Helen following "the hearse" to the grave site, buried her among remnants of ferns, grasses, and some garden poppies that had gone wild in the field.

Tosca was born on a blanket in the corner of my living-room—along with eleven brothers and sisters, all of whom made their careers elsewhere. Shamper's Bluff was the only home she ever knew, and she knew it well, much better than I. Although I can see as well as she could and, with my exceptional hearing, often felt that I could detect distant sounds as quickly, my nose was no match for hers. With a sense of smell at least one million times greater than mine, Tosca sniffed and accurately filed away information on every person who came up the driveway and, when spending an evening in the house, would bark a warning that a raccoon was crossing the back field or a squirrel was invading the woodpile in the porch. For years she took an early morning walk to the compost heap to learn who had been visiting during the night, and although occasionally she was not amused, usually she accepted the news simply as information that might come in handy later on. I often envied her natural composure, her sense that "this is how things are today," and hoped that one day I would be as well adjusted.

Tosca always seemed to know exactly where I would be pointing my camera lens next, and frequently took this as a cue that I needed a model. Once when I was composing a picture in the field behind my house, I was startled

A summer morning at Shamper's Bluff.

to observe two small brown triangles moving in tandem along the bottom edge of the viewfinder. I looked up quickly to see Tosca walking across the field, her ears protruding up into the picture space. Other times she wagged her tail or poked a paw into my composition precisely at the moment that I released the shutter. She seemed to know exactly what she was doing, and operated effectively at speeds of up to one-sixtieth of a second. For a long while I found her behaviour very annoying, but one day when I caught myself shouting at her crossly, I realized how well she understood me and what I was doing, and I was never cross with her again. Only those who know and care about you, and who feel comfortable about themselves, recognize the right moments for teasing you.

Tosca lying among the lupins along my driveway, Shamper's Bluff, 1994.

Although my relationship with Tosca typifies the quiet emotional sustenance I experience at Shamper's Bluff, this is also my place of business. It is where I make, edit, and file most of my photographs, where I create audio-visual sequences and assemble slides for teaching, where I bring participants from the workshops that I conduct nearby. It is also the place where the phone rings at any hour and the fax machine churns out sheets of paper, the place where I spend long nights sitting in front of my computer composing articles for photographic, motorcycling, and gardening magazines; writing and revising book manuscripts; developing and writing the menu for a CD-ROM; and imagining future projects—especially the creation of digital images from existing photographs. In these and other ways it is typical of many small-business addresses—a very ordinary place indeed.

Although I have been earning my living from photography (and writing) for over thirty years, I might have been a cinematographer, a painter, an actor, or, given a different body configuration, a dancer. In the most basic sense the particular profession or medium doesn't really matter, but what does matter to me—tremendously—is that I have been able to live and work in a medium and a manner that have allowed and enabled me to engage my emotions, to develop and use the right side of my brain along with my left, and gradually to begin the important work of connecting my conscious and unconscious selves. Photography has been the passport that enabled me to travel from the sort of life I expected into the kind of life I wanted.

Although I work long and hard because, for the most part, I love what I'm doing, I nevertheless experience times of significant emotional stress. Almost invariably I am warned by a dream that I am converting pressure into stress—before I am consciously aware of it. If I fail to heed the message, my body sooner or later reacts with minor or sometimes serious physical illness, which is a second warning.

Although I have to resolve personal stress within my human context, I can accomplish this goal more quickly and effectively when I stop being introspective for a while. I am convinced that our health and well-being as individual persons and as human communities depend on our willingness to engage regularly with the natural system that gave us birth. Exploring the natural world around me instead of focusing constantly on myself is the emotional equivalent of choosing a new camera position, rather than observing subject matter repeatedly from one point of view.

This conviction may seem irrelevant to many inner-city dwellers, but its relevance is immediately apparent on Shamper's Bluff, which is one reason why I acted to make this place an ecological preserve. Simply knowing that the plants and animals, and the air, soil, and water can continue to interact with one another as a healthy natural community brings me a peace of mind—perhaps more accurately, a peace of soul—that endures even during those times when I am grappling with personal difficulties and anxieties, and contributes to my healing process. Also, the continuous natural activity here sustains me emotionally. I am absorbed by my discovery of a crab spider camouflaging itself in the floret of a white lupin blossom as it waits for a winged meal to fly within pouncing range. Not being an eligible edible, I eventually pass safely by—only to be stopped seconds later by the flash of light from a pearl of water resting in the very centre of a lupin leaf. As I tilt my head, altering the angle of perceived light, the pearl becomes a prism—so I tilt my head at a different angle, and look again. An hour passes, two hours, or more, and during all this time I have forgotten about myself. When I become aware of the time again, I find that the "me cramp" that had hobbled me all morning has completely disappeared.

I love the deserts of southern Africa for the same reason. They shift my focus off myself so completely that the consciousness of self that remains is integrated with the sand and rocks. On several occasions I have felt so at one with the desert that I have wanted to lie on the sand until it absorbed me— the surfacing in my consciousness of a primal yearning to be reintegrated with the source of all being. Is this what coming home really means? Such an experience has never occurred in the hurly-burly of my normal, daily life, and I would prevent it from happening in the desert if I were to keep the focus on myself by carrying "civilization" along with me in the form of all sorts of extraneous creature comforts. So, except for a couple of bottles of good wine for celebration, Colla and I take along only what we need for survival, plus a little more in case we get stranded for a while. It's important to go as naked as possible.

My Shamper's Bluff environment and my sojourns in Canada, Africa, and elsewhere have convinced me that the experience of "wildness" in my life is an emotional necessity, indeed a spiritual one, which means that for me the continuous destruction of wild places represents a profound loss—akin, let's say, to the deliberate destruction of Mecca or the Vatican. I do not believe that every advance in culture depends on the conquering or bridling of nature, but rather that this pervading assumption of our industrial–technological society must itself be radically reformed—to be replaced by what Father Berry would call a new "human–Earth relationship" in which we would view all the materials and life forms of the planet not as a collection of objects, but as "a communion of subjects."

In the broadest and deepest sense, this communion is both my spiritual home now and my dream for the future of the planet. In this dream both the forests of Shamper's Bluff and the flowers of Namaqualand will have a voice. The dignity of the ocean will be recognized and its voice will be heard. A desert will be valued as a desert—not just as a mineral resource or a tourist destination. A bog will be important, and so will humans. We will be Earth aware. We will think and feel for the whole planet, and have a place and a voice that we have never had before.

One day in late November 1992, when I was having lunch with my parents at their home, my mother, who was eighty-seven and had all her wits about her, suddenly exclaimed, "I never expected to live so long!" Within a week she suffered a stroke and was admitted to hospital, where she died twelve days later. Her final days, marked by moments of holy togetherness, are the most exquisitely beautiful of my life. Less than a year later, when both my sister, Doris, and I were out of the country, my father, who had recently celebrated his ninetieth birthday, died instantly as he left the breakfast table.

On a sunny December afternoon a little while before Christmas, Doris, her husband John, and I buried the two urns containing the ashes of Ethel and Gordon Patterson. Both our parents had been remembered and honoured by the community at memorial services, but we had always known that their burial would be a private and very personal ceremony.

No amount of imagining had ever prepared me for the overwhelming sense of finality I experienced with the death and burial of my parents. Whatever had been said and done and felt between us is all that will ever be said and done and felt. It is over. They are gone. And yet . . .

My parents live on in my life in a thousand ways and appear frequently in my dreams. In one dream several months ago, when I was using a bulldozer to clear away a huge mound of garbage and other debris my father had dumped at the side of a road, I discovered at the very bottom of the pile a packet of shiny metal tools that he had left behind. And, just the other day, when I was trying to do two important jobs at once and becoming thoroughly stressed out, I recognized my destructive behaviour and sat down in an easy chair to relax my body and my mind. I was asleep in moments, and soon was dreaming of a small group of faceless human figures entering my front door. Suddenly my mother—beautifully groomed, her face no longer wrinkled, and wearing a lovely new turquoise coat—stepped out smartly from behind the others, looked directly at me, and held me with her smile. I exclaimed, "Mom, you've been away so long. It's so good to see you. You look beautiful." She just kept on looking at me—and smiling, and smiling, and smiling. Two wonderful gifts from my parents: some shiny tools from my father, and my mother's blessing.

And now, even Tosca has departed. The way she died seems to me a particularly natural conclusion to her life, but not an unusual one around here. Death is a daily, life-giving reality at Shamper's Bluff. The leaves are no sooner on the trees than insects of one sort or another are laying eggs or munching holes in them. As they fly away to another bush, tree swallows pick them out of the air. From my deck I can watch a kestrel swooping down on a mouse in the field below, or a red fox trotting through a grove of snowy pines with a limp hare in its mouth. Hot summer winds that quickly dry up puddles leave behind the tiny corpses of late-hatching tadpoles. October's falling leaves become the diet of bacteria and fungi.

Tosca has yet to return in my dreams, but she will. She is too important to me to stay away for long. Besides, the wild animals have moved in on her territory, and undoubtedly she will want to say something about that. Nearly every morning now the red fox emerges from the woods behind my house and trots across the field, passing within a metre or two of the front door as it continues on its way to its den in the pines below, but sometimes it pauses long enough to sniff the tires of my pick-up, just as Tosca might have done.

In the woods
behind my house,
Shamper's Bluff,
late 1980s—a
self-portrait.

The red squirrels are growing bolder by the hour—one came hopping along
the cedar steps in the garden yesterday, ostensibly for the purpose of smelling
the toe of my boot, but I suspect self-interest. A couple of white-tail does
graze on the last green lupin leaves outside the sun-room, or join the herd of
nine that sleeps at the foot of my driveway when it's not too windy and cold.
A pair of ruffed grouse hunt and peck in the grass beside the barn. So far,
I've made no attempts to photograph any of them. Just having them around
makes me feel happy.

  Nothing has liberated me as much or enabled me to enjoy my life more
than gaining a sure and certain sense of my mortality. The deaths of my
parents, my discovery of Tosca's body, even the dead grasses in which she
lay, and an illness of my own have helped me to accept death as my travelling
companion. I waste very little time now, compared with even a decade ago.
Moments count, and the quality of them even more. Every minute that I
spend worrying unnecessarily about "what the neighbours think," or
indulging my over-developed sense of obligation, or allowing myself to become
bogged down by the minutiae of every-day existence, I am diverting time and
energy from the privilege and the opportunities of living. Twenty-four years
have passed since I returned to Shamper's Bluff, but the process of coming
home to myself has been been going on even longer, and accelerating with

every year that passes. Even if I should live a long life, I no longer have a long future, and my greatest challenge—allowing my unconscious and conscious to operate in functional harmony—remains an uncompleted task. I still have important shadows to explore, but I have lost my fear of monsters that lurk in the dark—perhaps because the darkness is brighter than it was, more like travelling under a full moon than under a new one.

At every level, new experiences are rising from the ashes of old ones. My many new friends, for the most part, are decades younger than I. I love being with them and learning from them. Old friendships are ripening, deepening, and brimming with a wonderful sense of shared understanding and caring. My dreams are surfacing as never before—and I am remembering them and fitting them into my personal jig-saw puzzle. And, I feel a steadily growing courage to express my feelings and my thoughts honestly and without any embarrassment.

The energy of spring—here at Shamper's Bluff, or in my Namaqualand home, or wherever I may be—revitalizes me even more than when I was young, because it makes me feel the opportunity for growth. I try to plan my year's work, which normally involves travelling, to include as many springs as possible, but I always return to Shamper's Bluff in time to clean out the tree swallows' nests before the first scouts arrive in mid-April, and never accept assignments or engagements that would take me away from the sight of bilberries, wild cherries, and Canadian rhododendrons bursting into bloom in May, or the June spectacle of half a million lupins waving in the breeze along my driveway.

In one sense, I have come full circle, back to the area in southern New Brunswick where I was born and lived for the first eighteen years of my life. Back to the aromas of the forests and the sweet fragrances of the fields, back to the broad stretches of water that ripple through the meandering marshes of the lower St. John River and its tributaries, back to the mists that rise silently from the water surface and twist through the valleys in the golden morning light. Back to all the plants and animals I knew and loved as a child—my natural peer group and my friends. Have I returned home or come to one that I sought here, one that eluded me at the time? The truth, I feel, lies somewhere in between.

It's important for me to remember that I left here eagerly. It's also important for me to remember that I returned as eagerly as I had left. Although the community had changed considerably in seventeen years, the big change had taken place in me. I felt confident that I could claim my territory on my own terms. Or, to put it another way, I could be who I wanted to be, not who my parents or the community expected me to be. And the opposite was also true. With few exceptions, I could accept and value other people as themselves. Perhaps I had simply grown up.

My coming home is probably more like a spiral than a circle. A spiral rises as it curves back on itself; it is an ongoing creative process that, unlike a circle, will never be closed. I hope the spiral is, and always will be, the more accurate symbol for my life. My real home—the one I'm discovering through the process of travelling, questioning, reflecting, feeling, and photographing—is being myself in the communion of subjects.

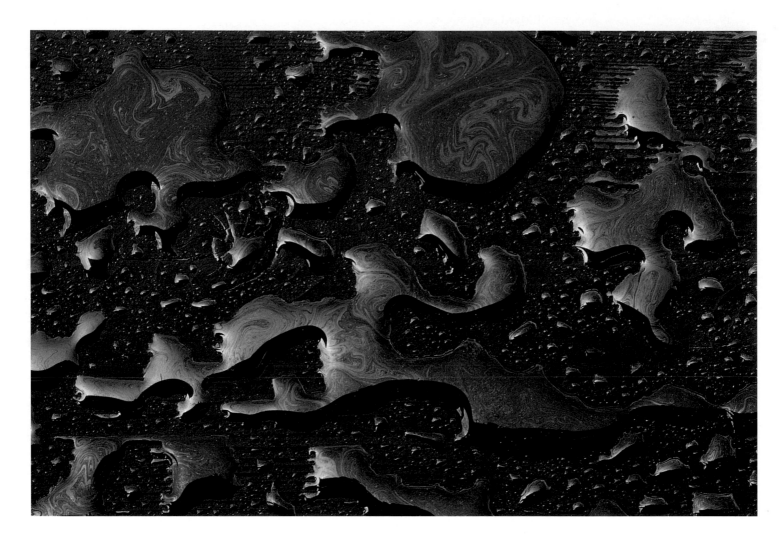

I probably make half of all my photographs at home. One day I spent several hours sitting on a bench, aiming my 100mm lens at waterdrops on a temporary deck. When the water evaporated, I sprayed the deck with my garden hose and kept on photographing.

Another day, wandering along a nearby beach before sunrise, I discovered a row of upturned kayaks that I abstracted into basic lines and shapes. I liked the way that the soft, indirect light, which cast no shadows, enhanced the saturated colours.

When I carry a camera with me to the river, which I usually do, I'm almost certain to use it. Only rarely do I set out with the idea of photographing a particular subject, preferring to let the water, aquatic plants, sand, stones, and reflected clouds capture my attention.

It's much the same when I walk along the old logging trail that begins near my house and wends through the woods down to one of the river's tributaries. Natural subjects abound in every season—tapestries of cedar twigs and spruce needles, clumps of ferns, sweeps of fragrant white violets, and animal tracks in the snow.

Tiny bluets carpet the fields around my house in late April and May. Although I frequently make pictures of overall displays, on damp mornings I often use a macro lens or other close-up equipment to zero in on one or two blossoms sparkling with dew.

Behind my house in late August and early September, I can still find an occasional lupin blooming among the grasses, most of which have lost even their patina of green. When I hear the telephone ringing in the distance, my mood begins to change from one of contentment to one of frustration. I have to decide which is more important. Frequently, I choose the flower.

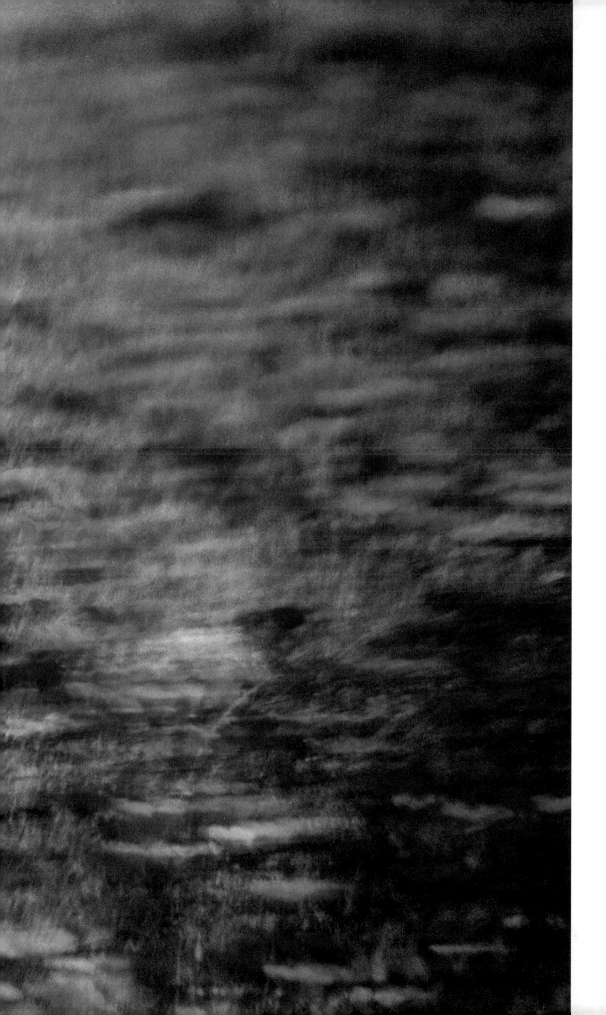

Walking past my barn, I catch a glimpse of my wildflower garden reflected in a pane of old glass. I elevate the legs of my tripod, change lenses, and begin the painstaking search for precisely the right camera angle and the most effective depth of field. By the time I press the shutter release, I have gained a new appreciation of Monet.

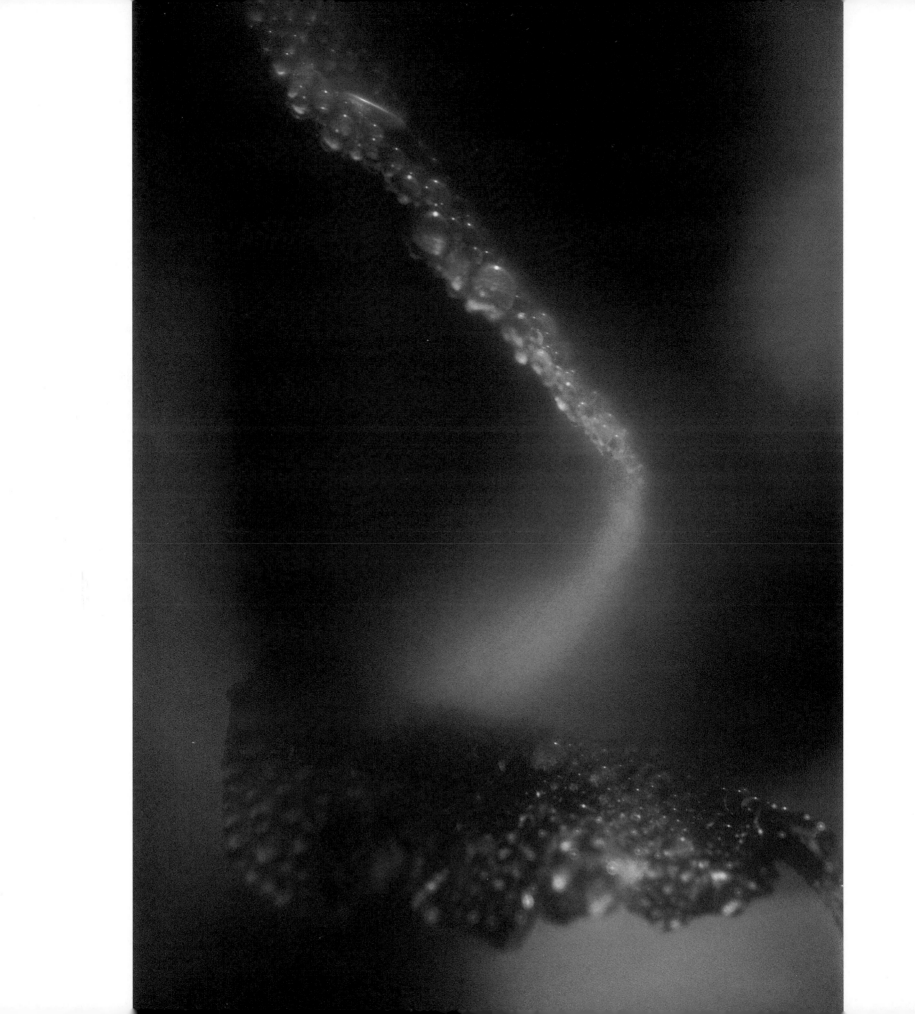

◀ Moving into the garden, I find myself influenced by the experience of photographing the flowers' reflection in the old window. Or, perhaps, by the little bluets in the spring. In any case, I have abandoned any notion that the literal is the whole of reality.

▶ Moments later I am creating and integrating visual elements only hinted at by the natural designs of leaves, flowers, and waterdrops. I am barely conscious of what I'm doing, but acutely aware of the euphoria that is pulsing through my whole body.

On misty mornings, for more than twenty years, I headed out the Shamper's Bluff road in search of the "best" locations for making pictures. Last year I would make a cup of tea instead, sit on my deck, and simply observe. I discovered that the opportunities for photographing light streaming through mist were as good at home as anywhere. The process of coming home to myself has been very similar—by quietly contemplating my feelings I've learned more about shadow and light than by racing around my emotional landscape.